Inland Tribes
of
Southern Africa

Basotho herdboy, Thaba Bosiu

Peter Becker

Inland Tribes
of
Southern Africa

Photographs by the Author

GRANADA
London Toronto Sydney New York

Published by Granada Publishing 1979

Granada Publishing Limited
Frogmore, St Albans, Herts AL2 2NF
and
3 Upper James Street, London W1R 4BP
1221 Avenue of the Americas, New York, NY 10020, USA
117 York Street, Sydney, NSW 2000, Australia
100 Skyway Avenue, Toronto, Ontario, Canada M9W 3A6
110 Northpark Centre, 2193 Johannesburg, South Africa
CML Centre, Queen & Wyndham, Auckland 1, New Zealand

ISBN 0 246 10926 2

Printed and bound at
William Clowes & Sons Limited
Beccles and London

Granada Publishing ®

To

DENYS HAY RANGER

Sukuma qhawe lakithi

Maps

Contents

Preface

In my previous book, *Trails and Tribes in Southern Africa*, I took my readers with me into the desert regions of southern Africa – Botswana, Namaqualand and Namibia and then, by way of contrast, to the luxuriant, well-watered eastern territories, from Mozambique to Swaziland and thence to KwaZulu and Transkei. In the present book we travel a network of trails in the central areas of the subcontinent. Invariably these are rutted, tortuous and almost impassable, because most of the inland tribal groups are mountain dwellers.

The trails I have followed in the course of twenty-five years have led to a host of exciting situations, as well as to innumerable people whose hospitality and generosity have made my involvement in field research an enduring and enriching experience. The pages of this book abound with examples of the cooperation I have received from chieftains, diviners, medicine men, village patriarchs, their wives, sons, daughters and friends. To all of them I say '*Maqhawe!*' which, literally, means 'Heroes!', but in a metaphorical sense serves to express my profoundest admiration and gratitude.

My very special thanks are due to Chiefs Kuini of Butha-Buthe, Letsie Theko (Thaba Bosiu), Nkuebe Peete MBE (Matsieng), Moroamache Sekhukhune (Mohlaletsi), Kgaba Moloto (Moletji), Boleu Rammupudu (Tafelkop), Nelwamondo (Venda), Vhavenda Netshimbupfe (Venda) and Raluswielo Mphaphuli (Venda). Also to Headmen Msiza II, Petrus Moloto, Nemagovhani, Ramulongo, Mathundinne and to the following respondents – Kopano Selomo, Clark Khetheng, Dixon Rafutho, Tseliso and Albert Khamelo, Pepetwana Skosana, Kgobalala Sekhukhune, Frans Phoko, Lucas Malatji, Paulina Lephalala, Ephraim Mulaudzi, Mishack Madavha, Norman Tshikororo, Frans Sandanu, Freddy Netshauba, David Nevhulaudzi, Boom Joubert and Dr Amy Jacot Guillarmod.

My sincerest appreciation to Connie, Harold, Peter, Nandi, Lindi,

Makoti, Monika, Simon, Shaun and Samantha for their consideration while I was writing at KwaVulindlela.

Finally, I am deeply indebted to Dina Odendaal, who 'insisted' on typing my manuscripts. An arduous task beautifully done...*mngane wami!*

PETER BECKER
KwaVulindlela
Bryanston
Johannesburg

Introduction

Apart from the Hottentots and Bushmen of the Western Cape, the indigenous peoples of southern Africa were virtually unknown to the outside world until the arrival of missionaries during the latter part of the eighteenth century. As a result of their carefully recorded observations, and especially the writings of the missionary explorers, John Campbell, Robert Moffat, Thomas Arbousset and David Livingstone, a handful of scholars began to focus their attention on the tribal groups of the distant interior. They were to make a comprehensive study of tribal cultures and vernacular languages, to gather fragments of history as narrated to them by tribal chroniclers and to seek out the biographical highlights of chieftains, medicine men and other imposing dignitaries. From their labours emerged a vast collection of letters, memoranda, published papers, journals and books – an invaluable storehouse of information.

In spite of the wealth of knowledge they accumulated, pioneer ethnographers and historians found difficulty in establishing the exact relationship between the tribal groups of southern Africa and the Negro peoples beyond the Zambezi river. What seemed to baffle them most was the multiplicity of languages spoken by Negro peoples throughout the continent. So although it was generally agreed that the southern African tribes were physically similar to other Negro Africans, it was also believed in certain quarters that they constituted a distinctive racial group. This theory was eventually dispelled on the strength of widespread research, which pointed not so much to the differences between southern African tribes and peoples in the north but to the linguistic, cultural and, especially, genetic similarities to be found among most people of Negro stock, throughout the length and breadth of Africa.

If the tribal groups of southern Africa are intimately linked racially to

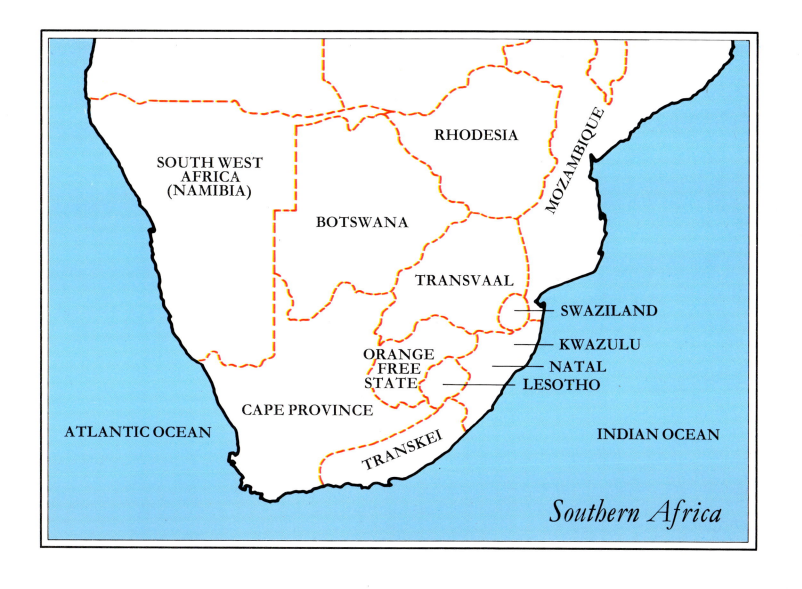

SOUTH WEST
AFRICA
(NAMIBIA)

RHODESIA

MOZAMBIQUE

BOTSWANA

TRANSVAAL

SWAZILAND

KWAZULU

ORANGE
FREE
STATE

NATAL

LESOTHO

CAPE PROVINCE

ATLANTIC OCEAN

TRANSKEI

INDIAN OCEAN

Southern Africa

the Negroes of Central and West Africa, how long have they inhabited the subcontinent? It is believed that some two thousand years ago Negro tribes, then living in the eastern regions of Central Africa, began moving gradually southwards as a result of a steady growth in population. The movement was a gradual process, a three-pronged expansion across the luxuriant and mountainous East Coast regions, the bush-clad flats and hills of the Northern and Western Transvaal and Eastern Botswana, the shallow valleys of the southern Orange Free State and the upper limits of Namibia. By 1770 the van of the Xhosa-speaking tribes had crossed the Great Fish river, and had come face to face with the White farmers of the Eastern Cape. Further large-scale expansion now came to an end, and tribes became acquainted with first the missionaries and then an increasing number of other White men – hunters, itinerant traders, travellers, adventurers and government officials.

Traditionally these tribal groups had pursued a peaceful way of life – tilling the soil, planting, weeding and harvesting crops, herding stock, attending feasts and observing age-old rituals and ceremonies. Admittedly there had been periodic squabbles between rival tribes over grazing rights or hunting grounds, as well as minor clashes between fighting men, mainly as a result of stock theft. Tribesmen first experienced the horrors of organized warfare when they came into conflict with Colonial forces. Then again in 1816, when Shaka the Zulu rose to power.

Having usurped the chieftaincy of the Zulu, one of a galaxy of similar East Coast tribes, Shaka, backed by a body of warriors called the *Izicwe*, surged through the territories flanked by the Pongolo, Tugela and Nyati rivers. He and his warriors then overran what is today Natal, Pondoland and much of Bomvanaland in central Transkei. Soon Shaka was proclaimed King of the Zulu, *Ingonyama* – the Lion – and supreme ruler over all tribes he had subjugated. No tribal chief had ever known such boundless power.

Although the great majority of defeated chiefs stoically acknowledged Shaka's paramountcy, three of them – Matiwane, Mpangazitha and Mzilikazi – absconded to the west in 1821, fearing he intended to kill them. Like Shaka, these three tribal rulers were destined to sow the seeds of internecine warfare in southern Africa. Even the far-off inland tribes would ultimately be driven by them into a maelstrom of chaos.

The Basotho

The present-day Basotho nation of central South Africa owes its existence indirectly to Shaka's emergence as a conqueror. When the chiefs Matiwane and Mpangazitha fled from KwaZulu, they led their followers along different routes into the slopes of the Drakensberg range. Having effected a crossing through the formidable peaks, and then descended into the western foothills, they entered the domains of the Sotho tribal group whose language they found foreign.

These peoples of the interior, the Zulu discovered, were timid and unaccustomed to war. They consisted of a mosaic of tiny tribes, each of which was independently ruled by an hereditary chief. The Sotho were tillers of the soil, planters of crops, hunters and cattle breeders. Indeed, their way of life would have been seen by the Zulu invaders as similar to their own, before King Shaka's rise to power.

With the arrival first of Matiwane and then Mpangazitha from across the mountains, a surge of fear swept the nearest inland territories, causing the local chiefs and their subjects to flee and scramble westwards into the dominions of neighbouring rulers. Soon the southern Orange Free State and Caledon valley swarmed with panic-stricken refugees who had abandoned not only their granaries but also their stock for the Zulu to seize. They were therefore forced to vie with each other for food and, as their numbers increased, they progressively denuded the environment of edible bulbs, roots, tubers, leaves, berries and fruits. They also wiped out every vestige of animal life – insects, birds, reptiles and game – with the result that hunger began to stalk them across every valley and plain and mountain slope. Children, pregnant mothers and the older folk fell out along the way and died. In the course of time, many thousands succumbed to famine.

Continuing westwards, the survivors pillaged the villages of fellow tribesmen who had not yet taken to flight. Squabbles broke out, armed struggles erupted and, to add to the mounting turmoil, Matiwane and Mpangazitha loomed continually over the eastern horizon. This led to internecine warfare and to *Difaqane* – an agonizing era that lasted eight long years, and reduced the once prosperous and peace-loving tribes to abject impoverishment and misery.

The wars of *Difaqane* left deep-seated scars in the minds of all who survived its horrors. Yet from its furnaces emerged the Basotho: an agglomeration of Sotho-speaking refugees tempered into a united group by a youthful visionary called Moshesh.

Ha Kuini Royal Village

Lesotho, land of the Basotho, is endowed with uncommon beauty, but is also subject to contrasting climatic conditions – generous rains, lingering droughts, broiling summers and icy winters.

Most of the Basotho inhabit a long, narrow belt of lowland territory skirted in the north and west by the Caledon river. The southern and eastern regions of Lesotho are sparsely populated. They consist of windswept and snow-capped mountain ranges, deep, sprawling valleys and a multiplicity of gorges, chasms and sandstone cliffs, streams, rivers and waterfalls.

In October 1955 I set out for Lesotho by truck, having spent much of the previous year in KwaZulu and northern Transkei. On arrival, I headed for Butha-Buthe, a sedentary hamlet founded in colonial times near the flat-topped hill after which it was named. Butha-Buthe hill, although relatively small and inconspicuous, stands out in Basotho history as a towering monument. For it was here that the young Moshesh first experienced the impact of *Difaqane* and the stage was set for the role he would play in founding the Basotho nation.

Before the outbreak of the *Difaqane* wars, Moshesh, son of a headman named Mokhachane, had lived with a handful of followers just north of Butha-Buthe hill. In the early 1820s, when news of the unrest in the east began filtering into the Caledon valley, he had moved to the summit of the hill, where he quickly established a village overlooking the lowlands. Access to Moshesh's new settlement was by way of an eroded dolerite dyke that had served during previous decades as a pass for both man and beast. There was a similar pass close by, and a third one on the opposite side of the hill.

I travelled to Butha-Buthe in 1955, specifically to visit the ruins of Moshesh's village. For a long time I had dreamt of standing among them, imagining the activities that had taken place there almost a century and a half before. The summit of Butha-Buthe meant far more to me than an ordinary hilltop. I agreed with the Basotho, who regarded it as hallowed ground.

Less than a stone's throw from the pass leading to the ruins I came upon Ha Kuini, royal village of Chief Kuini. Kuini, I had previously learnt, was a senior chief and a direct descendant of Moshesh. He was reputed to know every inch of Moshesh's village, and only with his permission could I climb the hill. Ha Kuini was not a big village. Its most conspicuous feature was a cluster of rondavel huts, their walls plastered with clay and cowdung and the roofs thatched with reeds. Fronting the huts was a tall, circular reed enclosure where the chief gave regular audience to his subjects, enjoyed the company of local cronies, and basked in the winter's sun sheltered from unfriendly winds. To the right of the huts was a rambling, rectangular cattlefold made of stones packed one on the other. There was also a sheep pen and a small enclosure for calves.

At the entrance to the village, I was met by a young dignitary named Kopano Selomo. When he learned I intended exploring the summit of the hill, he told me to wait at the truck while he announced my arrival to the chief. He then left me, returning about an hour later with news that the chief was unwell and unable to see me until the following morning. Chief Kuini, he added, had no objection to my visiting the ruins. In fact, provided he felt well enough, he was likely to act as my guide.

Selomo suggested we make an early start, not only because it was far to the ruins, but also because the chief might refuse to accompany me if I waited until the sun was too hot. He then bade me farewell and repaired to the interior of the village. I returned to a nearby hamlet where I was to spend the night at a local inn.

I was back at Kuini's village next morning just after seven o'clock, and was met again by Selomo. The chief, he told me, had recovered from his indisposition and wanted me to be taken to the reed enclosure. He, Selomo, had arranged for three horsemen to go with us up the hill, lest the chief should become fatigued and require a mount. I was delighted to learn that Kuini had decided to accompany us. I looked forward to meeting him.

No sooner had I been ushered into the enclosure by Selomo than the chief arrived. He was middle-aged, sparely built and a little stooped, and by the way he shuffled towards us, leaning heavily on a walking stick, he looked surprisingly infirm. Draped in a blanket, as is the fashion among the Basotho, he wore a conical straw hat, khaki trousers and heavy boots. As I stepped forward to greet him, he raised a hand in salute, and with no more than a hint of a smile muttered the customary Basotho greeting – *Khotso* – Peace. During these first few moments of our meeting, I concluded (quite wrongly as I was soon to discover) that he disapproved of me. There was an air of reservedness about him which I had not experienced before among chiefs, either in KwaZulu or Transkei.

Within the enclosure, to the left of the doorway, was an

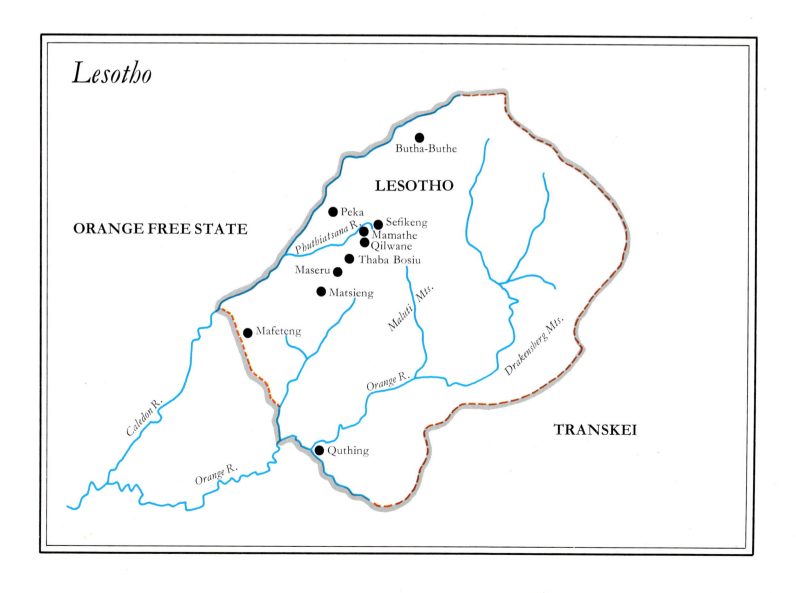

Lesotho

ORANGE FREE STATE

LESOTHO

● Butha-Buthe

● Peka

● Sefikeng

Phuthiatsana R.

● Mamathe
● Qilwane

● Thaba Bosiu

Maseru ●

● Matsieng

● Mafeteng

Maluti Mts.

Orange R.

Drakensberg Mts.

Caledon R.

Orange R.

● Quthing

TRANSKEI

Chief Kuini

Kopano Selomo,
a dignitary of Ha
Kuini village

open hearth, and beside it a ring of solid stools made from the fibrous trunks of the giant cactus (*Agave americana*) which grows in profusion in Lesotho. Seating himself at the far end of the hearth, the chief took a pipe from beneath his blanket. He lit it meditatively, then with a nod of the head indicated that Selomo and I should sit beside him.

At this stage, the three horsemen arrived, bowed to their chief and squatted on an ox-hide spread out near the hearth. For at least a minute we sat in silence waiting for Kuini to speak. As a greenhorn in Basotho territory, this was the quietest and longest minute I had ever known. Admittedly it was punctuated by the snorting of the horses, the crowing of roosters and bleating of goats and sheep. In addition, two snarling dogs paraded stiff-legged around a companion, watching it greedily gnawing a wedge of offal.

With a menacing swing of his stick Kuini drove the dogs away then, turning to Selomo, told him to assure me I was welcome at the Ha Kuini village. He said he would be happy to take me to the hilltop, and added that he was grateful Selomo had arranged for the horses to accompany us. Two could be used for riding, and the third for carrying food, water and sorghum beer.

Rising slowly, the chief left us without further comment. He soon reappeared, having changed his conical hat for an ordinary one. He now tapped the ground with his stick and, feigning impatience, cried: 'Come men, come let us go!'

Moshesh's Village, Butha-Buthe

The terrain between Chief Kuini's village and the foot of the pass is rocky, eroded and strewn with chips of stone washed down the hillside by rain. After fetching my cameras, a tape recorder and binoculars from the truck, we struck out in single file along a goat path, the horsemen leading the way. At an outcrop of lofty boulders we entered the pass, which shot suddenly upwards, swinging now to the left, now to the right, and then leap-frogging on to a broad shelf of rock. At this point the chief ordered a halt, perched himself on a stone and called to one of the horsemen for a mug of water. He was breathing heavily, his forehead, nose and goatee dripping sweat. He seemed distressed, and I could not help wondering if he would be able to climb to the summit. Next moment, however, he was plugging and lighting his pipe and filling the hot, still air about him with a screen of smoke. Then, tapping the ground with his stick, as he had done in the enclosure, he said: 'Come men, come let us not delay.'

The pass became really tricky now, growing steadily steeper, but also dropping into hollows, twisting between boulders and mounds of fallen earth, snaking through gullies and skirting miniature precipices. We had to measure every step we took, for the ground was loosely carpeted with gravel. I marvelled at the confidence the horsemen had in their mounts, as they inched their way into the heights. But of all horses bred in southern Africa none is as sure-footed and suited to mountain tracks as the so-called Basotho pony. A sturdy hybrid derived from Javanese, Arab and other strains, it is also uniquely adapted to the climatic extremes that sometimes plague Lesotho. The three we had with us never faltered as they negotiated the acute angles and acclivities of the pass. They became instinctively cautious over the smooth, rocky ledges and, where these were littered with stones, they cautiously tested the surface with their hoofs before going on.

During this second phase of the climb we stopped regularly for the chief to regain his breath and rest his legs. Eventually, at the top of the pass, we reached a wall of rocks which had been packed loosely together by Moshesh and his followers after the outbreak of *Difaqane*. The vastness of the summit now unfolded before us. Following a footpath on to a grassy shelf edged with sandstone scarps, we sat down together and shared a few mugs of sorghum beer. The morning sun pressed heavily upon us, and our ears throbbed with the chirping of crickets. The sky was cloudless, and the valley below was hazed with silvery heat. Lesotho cried out for rain.

So far the chief and I had barely exchanged a dozen words, and I felt the time had come to ask him about the importance of the hill in relation to the history of the Basotho nation. What better opening could there be than a reference to the weather? He was contentedly puffing his pipe, pausing now and then to wipe his sweating face, neck and hands and to fan himself with his hat. I switched on my tape recorder.

'It is hot today,' I began, turning towards him.

'Very hot,' he nodded.

'The country needs rain,' I continued.

'It needs rain, very much rain,' he replied. 'We haven't seen rain for over a year.'

'The lands down there in the valley,' I queried, 'do they belong to your subjects?'

'And also to me,' he said, 'and in the old days they were the lands of our ancestral father, Moshesh.'

'You know,' added Selomo, moving closer, 'whenever I climb this hill, and then look down the pass and across the

One of several walls built on the summit of
Butha-Buthe hill at the outbreak of the *Difaqane*
wars

valley, I tell myself it must have been hard in those times to
live.'

'Hard?' interjected Kuini. 'It was more than hard. What
could have been harder than to live day after day in fear? You
see, before the coming of the Zulu invaders, there had been
peace everywhere, not only in the highlands but also the
lowlands where most of the people had their villages.

'*Difaqane* brought confusion to these parts. Gentle people
were suddenly turned into runaways, robbers and killers and
finally some of them into cannibals. Strangely, it was not the
Zulu conquerors but the Batlokwa [Wild Cat People], our
own Sotho-speaking brethren, who first turned the lowlands
into a place to be feared. They were the biggest of the Sotho
tribes, and when they were put to flight by the Zulu, they
trampled the smaller groups underfoot in the rush. Those

Wild Cat People, led by their queen, the fearsome Mantatisi,
and her son Sikonyela, were merciless fighters. Not because
they had always been that way. Not at all. It was simply
because there were so many of them, and the menfolk had far
more women, children and elderly people to find food for
than had the men of Moshesh's small group, or others to the
west. Hunger was their biggest problem, and this together
with their fear for the approaching foe made them fierce and
merciless.

'It was lucky for Moshesh that he and his followers had
lived so close to Butha-Buthe hill. Because if they had not
wisely moved from the valley to the summit at the start of
Difaqane, they would have been destroyed by the Wild Cat
People, as others who remained in the lowlands were later to
die.

'It was this pass, the very one we have come up, and the other two, that did much to save them. Because, no sooner would the enemy warriors reach the higher parts, climbing one behind the other as we have just done, than they were driven back with a hailstorm of spears and rush of rocks. That was the purpose of the wall of stones which still stands at the top of the pass. Indeed, Moshesh planned many things on this hill as we will see. He was not one to be caught unprepared, no matter how cunning or how powerful the foe.'

Chief Kuini was in a mood for talking now, I told myself, watching him rise to his feet. Next moment, we were all back on the footpath, the chief leading the way and heading for the opposite edge of the summit. We had hardly walked fifty paces when he brought us to the ruins of stone-walled huts once occupied by Moshesh's sentinels.

'As you can see,' said Kuini, 'these were very small huts, and were occupied by no more than two men at a time. Just enough space for the warriors to store weapons and food while they guarded the pass, or to eat and sleep in when they came off duty. There were also reed and grass huts far larger than these, but they would have rotted or been eaten by termites long before I was born. So to find signs of them now is quite impossible.'

Approach to the northern entrance of Moshesh's
hill-top settlement

Beyond the ruins the footpath curled languidly into the northern side of a small, grassy elevation that dominates the otherwise flat-topped summit. Sprawled across the highest point were the tumbledown remains of Moshesh's old village. The huts, like those of the sentinels, were built of stones packed firmly together. They were, however, considerably bigger and the walls almost twice as thick. Grouped in crescent formation, they embraced what was once Moshesh's cattlefold – a circular stone-hedge enclosure flanked by a smaller one in which, presumably, calves were kept. Other ruins dotted the rise to the rear of the crescent. Some of these, according to the chief, had once been storage and cooking huts and others the homes of dignitaries.

We could find no trace of the rest of the settlement, the many homes known to have been occupied by Moshesh's retainers, warriors and servants; so we concluded they had been made of reed and other perishable materials, and had disintegrated in the course of the years, merging with the soily crest of the hill.

According to Chief Kuini, when the Wild Cat People were suddenly sighted by Moshesh's sentinels in 1822, panic swept the little hilltop settlement. The men had immediately taken up positions above the two north-facing passes, while the women, children and greybeards headed for the third one on

The first of the tumbledown sentinel huts

the opposite side of the summit. They crept a short way down the slope and, turning to the right into a narrow track, followed it to the base of the sandstone cliffs. There they entered two spacious caves and waited, bunched together in silence.

Finding the valley deserted and Moshesh's group safely perched on the hilltop, the invaders first set fire to the abandoned villages and then, towards evening, bivouacked in the vicinity of present-day Ha Kuini. When darkness fell, the valley resounded to the beating of drums, the animated chatter of Wild Cat warriors and the chanting of women. They seemed in no hurry to launch an attack on the hill.

Next day, the Wild Cat People stripped Moshesh's lands in the valley of grain. But they made no more than a half-hearted effort to climb the hill, before moving away to wreak havoc among tribes farther to the west.

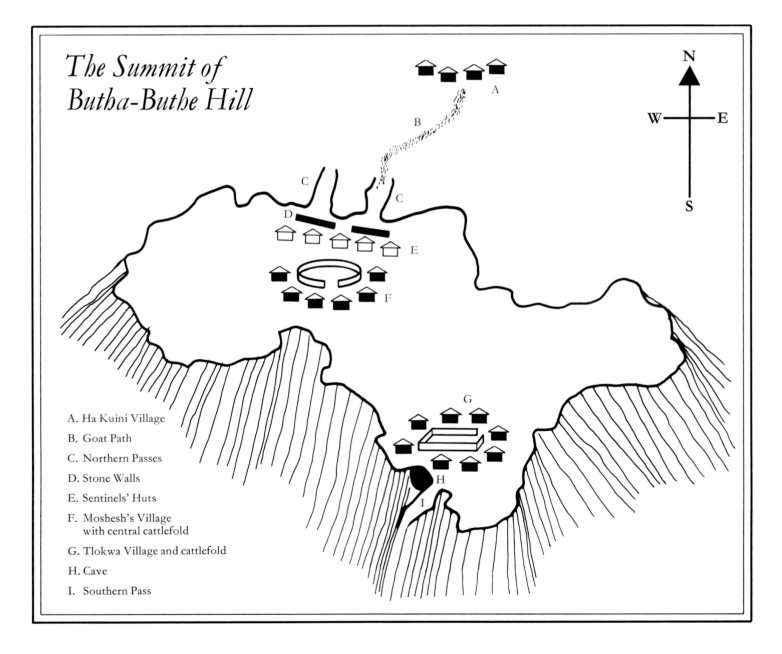

The Summit of Butha-Buthe Hill

A. Ha Kuini Village

B. Goat Path

C. Northern Passes

D. Stone Walls

E. Sentinels' Huts

F. Moshesh's Village
   with central cattlefold

G. Tlokwa Village and cattlefold

H. Cave

I. Southern Pass

Ruins of the village on the southern edge of the cattlefold

Site of the Tlokwa (Wild Cat) village

The Wild Cat Village

Towards its southern edge the summit of Butha-Buthe becomes progressively clearer of boulders and stony outcrops. Here Chief Kuini, Selomo, the horsemen and I came to the ruins of a second village. These were spread across a grassy flat overlooking both the pass and the caves where the women, children and aged men had taken refuge in 1822. One could see at a glance that it had been more recently inhabited. The hut walls were taller than those we had found at Moshesh's village, and were still covered in parts with plaster. In addition, some of the structures were rectangular in shape, an architectural style which developed after the arrival of missionaries in Lesotho in 1833.

'This is what remains of the homes of the Wild Cat People,' said Chief Kuini. 'The village was built by a section of Queen Mantatisi's subjects long after Moshesh and his followers had left the hill.'

After abandoning the attack on Moshesh's stronghold, Mantatisi and her hordes had laid the western lowlands to waste and then surged onwards into Botswana. There they had been dispersed first by the Ngwaketsi tribe in the region of present-day Kanye, and then by a force of Tlhaping (Fish People) mustered by Robert Moffat, a Scottish missionary stationed at Kuruman. Struggling homewards through the Orange Free State plains, they were intercepted by the Zulu conqueror, Matiwane, and driven into the Caledon valley. Eventually, after eighteen anguishing months, the Wild Cat People had found themselves back at the foot of Butha-Buthe hill. Sikonyela, the queen's son, was now in command. He decided to rest his forces before 'revisiting the hill-dwellers', as Chief Kuini put it, 'and relieving them of their granaries and cattle'.

'No matter how hard, or how many times they tried,' Kuini continued, 'the Batlokwa could not reach the top of the hill. They were driven back again and again, not by Moshesh's small party of warriors themselves, but by boulders that kept rolling and tumbling down the passes.

'This does not mean the Wild Cat People would not have succeeded sooner or later. Who knows? They must have realized that boulders would eventually become scarce on the hilltop. No, what really saved Moshesh and his people was that the enemy were suddenly attacked from behind, and then put to flight by new arrivals from KwaZulu – a runaway Zulu regiment headed by a commander named Sepetsha.

'We can be thankful that the Zulu didn't stay long in the valley,' said Kuini, 'because they were very skilled warriors and were just as hungry as all the other people roaming the lowlands. The real reason why they decided to leave the hill alone, so it is said, was because they were on the run like everyone else, and our father, Moshesh, cleverly sent them grain and slaughter cattle to make the journey ahead more pleasant for them. You see, Moshesh was a far-seeing man.'

'Very far-seeing,' I replied.

'Very, very far-seeing,' added Selomo.

'But you realize how greatly far-seeing he was,' continued the chief, 'when you consider that even before the return of the Wild Cat People, he had come to believe Butha-Buthe was not safe enough for his people. Yes, even before that time he had sent scouts in search of a hill that was bigger and flatter on top, where the cliffs were higher and unending, and the passes more difficult to climb.

'So, as soon as he learned that such a place existed, he moved westwards with his followers to a hill called Thaba Bosiu, choosing a little-known inland route through the mountains. That was the way he thought ahead. Indeed, as I've already said, it was only much later that some of the Wild Cat People came to live on Butha-Buthe hill. And here they remained until about twelve years ago.'

Because of its remoteness and isolation from the rest of the lowlands, the Wild Cat village had never grown into a large and important settlement. It was of little historical significance, so we spent no more than an hour rummaging among the ruins. In some of the huts we found chips of earthen pottery, and at the rear of one of the larger rectangular structures, a small pile of hoe-blades heavily blistered with rust. On the top of an ash heap, matted with devil thorns, we discovered a well-worn square of river shale which, presumably, had once been used for sharpening knives and assegai blades. Reaching what was left of the cattlefold, we found it throttled with grass and prickly weeds. It looked uninviting. I suggested we go in but Kuini refused.

'You go,' said the chief, 'and we'll wait for you at the gateway.'

'That's right,' Selomo added, 'you must go alone because Chief Kuini is tired, and we're thirsty and in need of sorghum beer.'

An unwelcome sensation crept over me as I brushed my way through the grass and weeds towards a pile of stones crested with a toothless cattle skull and the ant-eaten remains of a tree trunk. Inspired by a puzzling eeriness that hung over the place, I sensed I had unwittingly intruded on the burial place of the deserted village's dignitaries. No wonder my

The dome-shaped
cliff overlooking
the goat track
leading to the
cannibal cave

Eastern entrance to
the cannibal cave

companions had remained behind! I pressed on half-heartedly, and had just reached the stones when I came suddenly face to face with a cobra. Eyeing me suspiciously, it raised itself, cupped its hood and nervously flicked the air with its tongue.

A shiver rippled all over me and, forgetting the rule to keep calm and stand motionless in a situation such as this – snakes are said only to strike at moving objects – I leapt sideways, went stumbling across a patch of thatching grass, flung myself over the cattlefold wall and landed with a thud at the feet of two blanketed men. I rose sheepishly from the ground, and the strangers helped me pluck pieces of grass and tufts of burr from my clothes. They were friendly and sympathetic fellows, and so tactful as neither to appear amused nor to ask what had caused me to leave the old cattlefold so hastily. They had been searching since daybreak for a stray mule, one of them told me, and had found it dead among the ruins a few minutes before our 'unexpected meeting'.

During the remainder of the afternoon, Chief Kuini and the rest of us, including the strangers, sat talking outside the cattlefold gateway. Much of the discussion dwelt on the escapades of the great Moshesh, and we debated at length the horrors of cannibalism in those far-off times. Particularly fascinating was a detailed description by Kuini of an enormous cannibal cave in the west near Mamathe village.

'It was once the hiding place of the fiercest cannibals in all Lesotho,' said the chief, 'and fiercest of all was their leader, Rangotseng, a runaway Sotho dignitary.'

'It's a wonderful cave, and not difficult to find,' Selomo assured me. 'But in any case, it is known to everyone in and around Mamathe village.'

'So all you need do,' added Kuini, 'is to ask for Lehaha-la-Malimo (Cave of the Cannibals), and someone is sure to show you the way.'

Cannibalism

Cannibalism was unknown to the tribes of Lesotho before the 1820s and even then it was practised by a very small section of the population. It was adopted exclusively by hunger-tormented *Difaqane* refugees, and was widely abhorred, not least by some of the cannibals themselves.

On the seventh day after Moshesh and his followers had left Butha-Buthe hill for Thaba Bosiu, their newly-discovered hill-fortress, a party of stragglers was captured by cannibals and dragged away to a hiding place near Sefikeng. Among the victims were eleven children, one of Moshesh's sisters, two of his wives and his grandfather, Peete. A party of warriors sent to track down the cannibals succeeded in retrieving the women and children, but by the time they arrived old Peete and others had already been killed and eaten.

The loss of the old man not only grieved Moshesh but caused him deep concern. Some years before, an elderly seer named Mohlomi had predicted that, provided he took care of old Peete, protected him from harm and eventually personally administered the customary rites at his burial he, Moshesh, would in turn be protected by the ancestral spirits and endowed with prosperity and supernatural powers. How would the ancestors react to Peete's death? Moshesh pondered. Would they ever be appeased, considering the way he had died and the fact that he had been deprived of burial? Suddenly the young chief saw a way out of the dilemma: if the cannibals were regarded as living sepulchres, he could perform the rites, as mentioned by the seer, over their stomachs.

So Moshesh had them captured, made them lie down side by side in rows, and rubbed moist, warm *mosoang* (intestinal manure of a ritually slaughtered ox) over their naked bodies. He then made contact with the shades of the dead in prayer, calling upon the ancestors to bless old Peete's spirit and imbue it with the power to communicate with him, Moshesh, in times of misfortune. After the ceremony, he treated the cannibals to a feast and, assuring them of his forgiveness, had them escorted back to their lair. In years to come, these and several other cannibal bands were accepted by Moshesh as his subjects, and in due course they ranked among the most loyal and law-abiding inhabitants of Lesotho.

The Cannibal Cave

I set out from Butha-Buthe for Mamathe on the morning after climbing the hill. On the outskirts of the village is the trading station owned by Charlot Jacot Guillarmod, grandson of a Swiss missionary who had settled in the area in 1872. Charlot, I had been told at the inn in Butha-Buthe, was the territory's foremost entomologist, and his wife, Dr Amy, its foremost botanist. Both had made a thorough study of Basotho culture and history, which included delving into the reasons for cannibalism during the previous century, and regularly visiting the Lehaha-la-Malimo.

I called in at the trading station, and spent two hours with them. When they learned I intended going to the cave, they arranged for a guide to accompany me. It lies hidden in the side of a north-facing sandstone escarpment and overlooks an immense valley which merges in the distant south with the foothills of the Maluti mountains. To reach it we travelled about seven kilometres by truck along a dusty track, and then on foot through a narrow fissure over-arched with boulders, trees and entangled shrubs. Linking up with a goat path, we went downwards, veering to the right across a bulge in the escarpment. We had to calculate each step for fear of slipping, and to avoid overbalancing we were forced occasionally to continue on our behinds, sliding feet first over treacherous rocks and mounds of earth.

At the bottom of the path we suddenly arrived at a long sandstone rock which beckoned us onwards through the folds of a towering dome-shaped cliff. We now crawled farther down the slope and, turning right again, saw before us the gaping mouth of Lehaha-la-Malimo, the cannibal cave. It was enormous. Far wider and higher than I had expected it to be. I estimated its area as roughly equivalent to a cluster of fifty Basotho huts. No wonder this particular cave had been chosen by Rangotseng's cannibals as a hiding place.

Below us was a chasm three hundred metres deep. Covered from side to side by a chaos of bush and cactus, and hazed with trembling heat, it had an air of silent foreboding. After scanning it for several minutes, we crept upwards through the rocks and into the cave. We found it swarming with hundreds of starlings and crows noisily squabbling over the remains of a goat. They scattered at the sight of us, filling the surroundings with a cacophony of screeches and a flurry of wings. A reverberation of echoes ricochetted through the cave, and I remember shuddering as I imagined the voices of the cannibals, the lamentations of their victims and the haunting atmosphere that must have pervaded this place many years before.

As we went deeper into the cave, a strange uneasiness crept over me, and a graveyard coldness shivered down my spine. Peering ahead across the grey inhospitable interior, I recalled my discussion with Charlot and Amy Jacot Guillarmod at the trading station. Long before Moshesh's time, they had told me, the cave had been inhabited by Stone Age hunterfolk. Charlot's grandfather, the pioneer missionary, Frédéric

Kohler, had come across a large variety of Bushman artifacts there – stone flints, arrowheads, scrapers, adzes and ostrich eggshell beads. He had also found human skulls and skeletal bones which he concluded were the remains of the cannibals' victims. He had sent these, and the artifacts, to the Musée de l'Homme in Paris. In more recent times Charlot and Amy had found similar evidence of cannibalism in the cave and the chasm below it. They had delivered a skull and several human bones to the local chief for interment in the burial grounds of Mamathe village.

My guide and I had not spoken to each other since entering the cave, and I wondered if he had sensed my reaction to the eerie surroundings. In any case the air was so stagnant now, and so heavy with the stench of decaying goat droppings and urine that carpeted the floor, that I struggled to breathe, let alone talk.

When we reached the far end of the cave, my guide drew my attention to a disarray of flat-top stones. 'This was the cannibals' kitchen and pantry,' he said, 'the place where they killed their captives and cut up the corpses for cooking. It is also the place where food was stored…and a place I hate to visit.

'When I was a boy,' he continued, 'our grandparents used to tell us about these stones. For very many years they were dark with the stains of blood…mainly brown, and in places black.

'The stains have worn away now,' he concluded, 'which makes me feel glad. We of Mamathe village have no wish to be reminded of those dreadful days; and the bloodstains that made forgetting impossible.'

I started photographing the interior of the cave, and as we slowly retraced our steps across the interior, I realized the chasm below was not as quiet as I had thought. For now I could hear bird song in its distant depths and the echoing chatter of women who had entered the bush in search of firewood. I could also hear the remote braying of donkeys, the lowing of cattle and the bleating of goats. I wondered why I had been deaf to all these sounds before.

I was to return to Lehaha-la-Malimo, Cave of the Cannibals, four years later and then again in 1965, but the visit that I remember most lucidly is the first one. On that occasion my emotions were moved beyond my comprehension. It was as if I had to be made aware of the intangible influences that permeate a place such as this: where so few people have lived, yet so many have died.

The central section of Lehaha-la-Malimo

Thaba Bosiu

No place in the whole of Lesotho is more steeped in history or representative of Basotho culture than the settlement of Thaba Bosiu. I left Mamathe in October 1955 to explore this flat-top hill where the Basotho nation had been founded.

At Thaba Bosiu I called on Letsie Theko, the most senior chief in the area. Like Chief Kuini of Butha-Buthe, he was a direct descendant of Moshesh. He was then thirty-two, a quiet, amiable man and, while I remained at Thaba Bosiu and, indeed, in later years, he encouraged me to research in the area over which he ruled. Cannibalism was a topic he had heard discussed by elderly chroniclers since early childhood, he told me, and to my delight he offered to share their views with me.

He began by recounting the capture and killing not only of old Peete, Moshesh's grandfather, but also of other dignitaries and innumerable commoners. As to the causes and results of cannibalism, he assured me his views were shared by all thinking Basotho.

'Most peoples,' the Chief began, 'have some part of their history they would like to forget, and would prefer outsiders not to know about. In our case, it's cannibalism. Present-day Basotho find it difficult to believe there were people in this land who once ate human flesh, and yet not so very difficult when they realize there were no cannibals before the *Difaqane* wars, and very few when the wars were over and traditional foods were again available. It was hunger and the fear of dying that caused some of our ancestors' heads to turn with that kind of madness – no stock, no crops and plenty of running away. Running and hiding day after day, and often at nights when they should have been sleeping.

'I can remember well our old people talking about the Kholokwane, the Phuthing and other cannibal bands that used to roam this part of the lowlands. Before *Difaqane*, they had lived in peace and had known very little about fighting and killing. There had been no reason for killing other human beings.

'Then came the time when the children began crying, all the time crying and pleading for food; and the menfolk, seeing them cry and become thin and feeble, were afraid their little ones would soon die. At the same time, those men saw their very own mothers and fathers silently weeping; not so much because of hunger, but because they were unaccustomed to so much fleeing and wandering, and their legs had become weak and shaky and swollen with pain.

'Just think of the hurt in the hearts of everyone, when eventually the old ones started falling out along the way, unable to continue, and slowly dying. And there were others dying – babies, ailing and crippled folk, pregnant women and, indeed, some of the younger men.

'And with all this dying taking place, eyes that had never seen food in human flesh, suddenly saw in human corpses a way of keeping alive. But never the corpses of relatives! Never! Only those to be found in the trails of other wandering bands. This was how cannibalism began.'

Chief Letsie now paused to greet and welcome an elderly councillor who had arrived on horseback to confer with him. Invited to join us, and learning of my interest in cannibalism, the councillor soon entered into the conversation.

'Our people talk a lot among themselves about cannibalism,' the old man said, turning to me, 'but usually not much with strangers. And often the ones that know least talk most, adding their own imaginings to appear knowledgeable.

'We Basotho enjoy a story well told, and our narrators compete with each other in the art of telling. So when I think of the many years that have passed since those early times, I believe that what is being said about cannibalism today is not altogether true to what happened then.

'A good example is the description of Rakotswane, the most powerful and feared of all cannibal chiefs. He is said to have been a very big man, to have had a very big stomach and a head much bigger than anyone else's. His mouth and teeth were said to have been twice the usual size and his eyes, shaded by thick, bushy brows, to have glowed like fire.

'I don't believe Chief Rakotswane looked like that. No, this is how he was made to look by many generations of grandmothers, who have always been our best storytellers. They knew, as I have already said, that the Basotho enjoy a story well told, so they turned Rakotswane into something he wasn't. In fact, there are only a few things about cannibals we can say with certainty:

'For instance, we know they had no real taste for human flesh and, knowing they were sinning, but unable to stop, spent much of their time in prayer, pleading forgiveness. Their sufferings taught them also to pray for mercy, and because they had many enemies and lived in fear, they prayed hard and long for protection.

'This meant they were more often in touch with the world of ancestors than they would otherwise have been. Which is perhaps why so many of the cannibals, when eventually

The councillor at
Chief Letsie's
village

pardoned by Moshesh, and given the right to settle in the valleys around Thaba Bosiu, were found to be skilled diviners and seers. It very definitely explains why almost all cannibals turned out to be humble, gentle and law-abiding when, in fact, the opposite had been predicted by Moshesh's advisers.

'When I think or talk about these things, as I seldom want to do, I feel a hurt within me. The *Difaqane* wars brought misery to the entire Lesotho, and most of all to those of our brethren it turned into cannibals.'

With these words the councillor brought the discussion to an end. Next moment, he was nonchalantly lighting his pipe and complaining to the chief about the drought and the poor condition of his stock. These topics were closer to his heart than cannibalism.

Basotho Villages

The settlement at Thaba Bosiu is rivalled in beauty only by Matsieng – Place of Locusts – forty kilometres to the south-west. These are the two most important villages in the history of Lesotho. Not only did they feature prominently in Moshesh's eventful career, they also cradled his lineage, including the distinguished rulers who succeeded him. Thaba Bosiu and Matsieng have even more in common: each is sprawled across the base of a hill, facing roughly northwards on to fertile valleys where the crops are grown and the animals pastured. They are also two of the biggest villages in the Lesotho, consisting of hundreds of home-steads and family units bonded to a greater or lesser extent by kinship ties.

I researched in Thaba Bosiu and Matsieng during the fortnight following my discussion on cannibalism with Chief Letsie and the councillor. I had planned to visit Moshesh's hilltop fortress at Thaba Bosiu without delay, but as the guide Letsie had earmarked for me was away at the time, I was advised to postpone the climb until he returned.

Since those far-off years, I have returned frequently to Thaba Bosiu and Matsieng. I have also worked in numerous other Basotho villages, some of them in the very heart of the highlands. As in the case of Thaba Bosiu and Matsieng, they are found mainly in areas where the soil is suitable for tilling and planting, where grazing is plentiful and where water is always available. Most of the villages are situated on the northern slopes of mountains and hills, for in this way they are protected against the whims of the wintry winds that blow from the south.

Villages vary considerably in size. They may consist of no more than a handful of homes occupied by one or two family units. On the other hand, they may extend over vast areas, the number of inhabitants varying from a hundred to several thousand.

Basotho homes are either round or rectangular in shape, and are built of reeds, stones or home-made bricks. They are roofed with reed or thatching grass, and not infrequently with sheets of corrugated iron. The inner walls are usually plastered and painted with red, brown or yellow clay. In addition, they are often adorned with drawings of animals, birds, reptiles and flowers, and the outside walls with geometric patterns scratched into the drying surface, or with river pebbles pressed firmly into the daub.

When the French missionaries, Eugene Casalis, Thomas Arbousset and Constant Gosselin, arrived in Lesotho in 1833, they found the great majority of inhabitants living in 'sparrow-nest' huts. These homes were made exclusively of grass or reeds fixed to an oval framework made of staves. Compact and cosy, they were entered through a short, tubular passage which served in winter to protect the occupants from unfriendly winds. Today this style of hut has virtually disappeared, although traces of its influence can be seen in Matsieng and other major villages, where numerous homes made of stone or brick are oval in shape and fronted with projecting entrances.

Clusters of homes constituting a village household are often isolated from adjoining families either by low, stone walls, reed hedges or rows of aloes. Huts vary in size. The larger ones are used as living rooms, dining rooms and sleeping quarters and the others as storage places for foodstuffs, utensils, tools, blankets, skins and clothing. The younger children and infants sleep with their parents, and adolescent girls with their grandmothers. Youths are accommodated in a special hut under the supervision of adult males.

Basotho Cattle

The Basotho are assiduous pastoralists; villages resound continuously to the bellowing of cattle and the bleating of sheep and goats. They also keep fowls, donkeys, mules, pigs, dogs and cats and, of course, horses which they count among their most prized possessions.

Homesteads along the base of Thaba Bosiu

The north-western limb of Thaba Bosiu

Like virtually all other tribal groups of southern Africa, the Basotho look upon cattle as a yardstick for measuring wealth and prestige. They have an intense love for their herds, and when men sit together in conversation over a pot of sorghum beer, they enjoy discussing the condition of their oxen, the fertility of their cows, the virility of their bulls and the number of calves recently born.

In all tribal societies and, indeed, in the rural areas of Lesotho, cattle fulfil a multiplicity of functions. For example, not only are they the main source of dairy products and constantly used as draught animals, but their hides are turned into mats, shields, thongs and items of clothing. Cow- and ox-tails are fashioned into fly-switches, horns into receptacles, snuff-boxes and musical instruments, and tail hairs into plaited ornaments. Even dung is put to use in several ways: it is unsurpassed as a fuel for cooking, and mixed with mud or clay serves as an outstanding binding agent for bricks and plaster. It is also used by the womenfolk for sealing the lids of earthen utensils, and by medicine men for treating sprains, abrasions, bruises, cuts and swellings.

Cattle play an important role in other ways. In traditional law and justice, for instance, they constitute the prime medium for settling fines. In marriage, they form the basis of *mahadi* or marriage goods which have to be provided by the groom before the impending union can be validated and the wedding ceremony arranged. They are also used extensively in rituals and ceremonies, being ranked above goats and sheep as sacrificial animals. Indeed, should misfortune strike a tribe as a whole, or should there be reason for widespread celebrations, it is customary for an ox to be offered in sacrifice to the realm of ancestors. Only on less significant occasions are goats or sheep regarded as adequate.

In Thaba Bosiu and Matsieng and, in fact, in all parts of Lesotho, much time is devoted to the care of cattle. The cows are milked by herdboys in the mornings and again at sunset, and are grazed in the outlying pastures or harvested grain fields during the rest of the day. Towards midday they are watered at the nearest stream or spring, and in the late afternoon are returned to the stone-walled cattlefolds among the huts.

Basotho herdboys have a deep affection for the cattle assigned to them by the men of the villages, and take pride in their ability to identify their charges at a glance according to distinctive colourings, markings, shapes of horns, scars and other physical characteristics. By the time they reach adolescence, the herdboys will have memorized innumerable terms descriptive of cattle. For example: *e chitjana* – the cow without horns; *e kgumwana* – the red cow; *e phutswa* – the black ox with white spots; *e tsebe enngwe* – the ox (or cow) with one ear; *e selota* – cattle with humps. Add to these terms for cattle diseases, as well as the enormous vocabulary connected with the cattlefold, milking, taboos, and, indeed, cattle breeding in general.

Village Activities

Activities in villages throughout the lowland regions follow a similar pattern. At Thaba Bosiu, for example, the day begins at the first light of dawn, and is accompanied by the bellowing of the herds, the bleating of goats and sheep, the yapping of dogs, the squawking of crows, the chirping of sparrows and finches and the piping of doves. As the villagers emerge from their huts, the women start lighting the fires for the morning meal. The men, meanwhile, inspect their stock in the cattlefolds and pens, while the children frisk noisily around the courtyards, or go rummaging through the previous night's cooking pots for titbits of food.

Agricultural activities such as tilling, planting, hoeing and reaping begin soon after sunrise, and continue throughout the day until dusk. Much of this work is done by the women, because invariably a large percentage of the menfolk are away from home, having taken jobs in nearby towns or in industrial areas outside Lesotho.

After the day's work, fires are kindled and the evening meals prepared either by the mothers of households or their teenage daughters. The boys, meanwhile, have milked the cows and tightly secured the cattlefold gates. They have also made sure that the fowls have gone to roost in the trees or have settled on the tall, four-legged platforms built specially for their protection against dogs and genets. Eventually the family gathers at the fireside to eat and discuss the day's events. Very often the evening meal is followed by dancing and singing to the strains of a guitar or concertina.

This brings to mind my brief meeting with Ezekial Theko, a young man who was reputed during the 1950s to be the finest guitar player not only in Thaba Bosiu, but also the villages as far afield as Quthing. I can see him now during my visit to Thaba Bosiu. He was seated on a lofty boulder, his body draped in a scarlet blanket patterned with rampant crocodiles, and his face shielded by a conical straw hat from the slanting rays of the afternoon sun.

Basotho cattle are named according to their
colouring, markings and shape of horns

I had been strolling through the village among goats and
sheep and squalling children when suddenly I halted and
listened, spellbound to the strumming of Ezekial's guitar. At
that moment, scores of youths and maidens came surging
forward from all directions, their faces reflecting intense
delight. Soon the spectators began to clap their hands to the
rhythm of the music, and then to sing and dance, kicking up
whirls of dust. It was a riot of merriment. And later, when a
procession of leaden clouds came floating in from the south,
belching lightning, thunder and a deluge of rain, more
villagers arrived to take part in the dance – children, mothers
with infants strapped to their backs and greyheads stooped
with age.

'*Pula! Pula!* – Rain! Rain!' they cried, turning their faces
to the heavens, baring their shoulders and snatching at the
raindrops that cascaded about them with outstretched hands.

Within minutes the rain had stopped and the sun shone
through; ground that had been thick with dust was churned
into a layer of mud. The dancing lasted for at least an hour,
and would undoubtedly have continued had two of Ezekial's
guitar strings not snapped and his playing come to an end.
Even so, long after people had dispersed and returned to
their homes, I could still hear them singing Ezekial's songs.

In addition to singing and dancing, a popular pastime in
Basotho villages is an indigenous game called *marabaraba*.
Akin to draughts, it is played by two opponents using a
homemade board made of plank, cardboard or even a slab of
sandstone.

The players begin with twenty-two 'cattle', represented by
eleven river pebbles on one side and eleven peach pips on the
other. The principle involved is for the opposing 'cattle' to

outmanoeuvre and then 'devour' each other. The game comes to an end when one of the players has been totally bereft of his 'herd'.

Apart from *marabaraba*, adult Basotho sometimes play card and dice games after evening meals. This is also the time when the children romp around the huts, or are treated by an elderly member of the household to a bedtime story. By nine o'clock, however, few of the villagers are still astir, for it is customary in rural areas for everyone to retire early to bed. Sleep itself is a cherished pastime – especially during the winter.

The Hill of Destiny

On the morning of the last Sunday in October, I received news from Chief Letsie that the guide appointed to take me to Moshesh's hilltop fortress had returned and was waiting for me to contact him. I was to meet him at a nearby mission station, where some of the villagers had assembled to pray for rain.

The stone church in front of the mission station was one of the oldest buildings in Lesotho, erected by the French missionaries, Casalis, Arbousset and Gosselin in 1837. Reaching it, I was enthralled by the sound of scores of voices blended in four-part harmony. The worshippers were singing 'Abide with Me', my favourite hymn, in the vernacular. I sauntered to a gigantic syringa tree beside the church, and seated myself against its trunk. Slowly my thoughts filtered back to the days of Moshesh's rule, and the unfolding of his destiny on the summit of the hill, Thaba Bosiu. I became steeped in reverie.

Nine days after leaving Butha-Buthe hill in 1822, Moshesh and his weary followers reached the eastern side of Thaba Bosiu, and marvelled at its precipitous slopes and the unending procession of sandstone cliffs that lined the summit. Pressing on, they reached the western limb of the hill at sundown, and then started to climb. Slowly and cautiously they struggled up a craggy pass called Khubelu, their feet aching, their bodies racked with fatigue.

Cowdung is mixed with water to form a mash. It is then dried, cut into squares and used as fuel for cooking

Basotho fowl roost

overlooked yet another pass which the newcomers were appropriately to name after old Mokhachane.

For some time Moshesh and his people lived in makeshift huts, in caves and under ledges of rock. While the two main settlements were being built by handpicked craftsmen, the rest of the community was employed in fortifying the Khubelu, Ramaseli and Mokhachane passes. They collected rocks along the slopes, some flat and jagged, others round and smooth, and stacked them into mounds along the fissures and cliffs through which the passes meandered. They then fortified the three remaining passes of the hill – the Mahabeng, the Raebe and Makara.

No sooner were they established on Thaba Bosiu than Moshesh and his people were attacked by small bands of *Difaqane* marauders, whom they were able to repulse without difficulty. They were also regularly visited by hunger-crazed refugees to whom Moshesh gave not only food, but also permission to live on the hill. More and more suppliants found their way to Thaba Bosiu. Indeed, by 1824 Moshesh's followers had increased so considerably he was compelled to settle all newcomers in the valley within easy reach of the Khubelu pass. Three years later, an estimated three thousand people were settled on the summit, with almost as many near the base of the hill. In 1829 they began referring to themselves as the Basotho, or Sotho people, and to Moshesh's new domain as Lesotho.

During the following four decades, as the population multiplied and villages sprang up throughout the lowlands, the Basotho were frequently attacked by powerful foes – the army of Matiwane, the Zulu invader; Koranna, Griqua and other half-caste *banditti*; Matabele regiments of the hitherto invincible conqueror, Mzilikazi; a British expeditionary force under command of Sir George Cathcart and finally, on two occasions, by Boer commandos.

Many black, brown and white fighting men were to perish on the slopes of Thaba Bosiu, in fact not a single invading army succeeded in reaching the summit. Moshesh's foes were always humiliated by the unorthodox tactics employed by the hill's defenders. They had no effective method of countering the devastating rain of boulders, assegais and gun slugs that burst upon them whenever they ventured into the passes.

Moshesh's role as the benefactor of *Difaqane* refugees, the unifier of scattered Sotho tribes and the founder, father and supreme chief of the Basotho nation earned him considerable fame not only in southern Africa, but also abroad.

On the day after their arrival on the summit, Thaba Bosiu became a hive of activity. While Moshesh, old Mokhachane, his father, and the elders looked around for residential sites, the women went under guard to the nearby valley in the north, where they cut reeds and thatching grass along the banks of the Phuthiatsana river.

The spot eventually selected by Moshesh for his own homestead was situated some six hundred paces from the top of the Khubelu pass, and in line with the Ramaseli pass on the opposite slope of the hill. His father had chosen a site on the south-western bulge. Flanked by menacing precipices, it

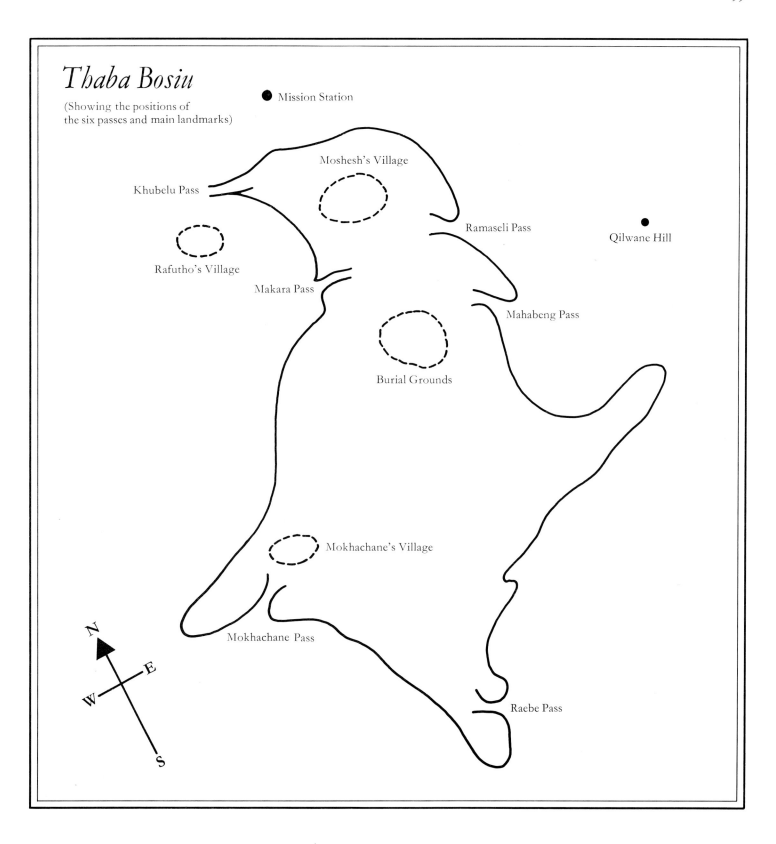

Thaba Bosiu

(Showing the positions of
the six passes and main landmarks)

Mission Station

Moshesh's Village

Khubelu Pass

Ramaseli Pass

Qilwane Hill

Rafutho's Village

Makara Pass

Mahabeng Pass

Burial Grounds

Mokhachane's Village

N

E

W

S

Mokhachane Pass

Raebe Pass

In the years between his rise to prominence and his death in March 1870, he was visited regularly by people from various walks of life – Zulu, Xhosa and other tribal dignitaries; white hunters, explorers, scientists, missionaries, runaway sailors, smugglers and itinerant traders; Boer emissaries and presidents; British royalty, government officials, generals and high commissioners. Such was the prestige of the great Moshesh and of Thaba Bosiu, his flat-topped Hill of Destiny.

The guide who was to take me up the hill found me lost in thought under the syringa tree beside the old mission church. Introducing himself as Clark Khetheng, he apologized for keeping me waiting. He had been praying for rain, he said, adding with a chuckle that prayers were seldom short in Lesotho: they took time, very much time.

Khetheng was a short, spindly, elderly man, with a haggard look that suggested he had weathered many storms of life. He had narrow, melancholy eyes, a broad, triangular nose, heavy lips, saggy cheeks and closely-cropped, greying hair. Clad in a floral, ash-grey blanket, baggy trousers and heavy boots, he held a Bible and hymn book in one hand and a stick in the other. From the very start I found him amiable, and eager to share the information he had gathered over the years about Moshesh's stronghold. No sooner had I risen from the ground and shaken his hand than he climbed into my truck and suggested we set out for the Khubelu pass.

We followed a rutted track along an avenue of towering aloes, threading a way between huts and cattlefolds and flocks of goats. Turning left along the base of the hill, we reached the village of a patriarch called Dixon Rafutho whose great-great-grandfather had lived on that very spot a century before, and had served Moshesh as a blacksmith.

Marabaraba, an indigenous game played on a slab of sandstone

The terrain westwards of the Khubelu pass

From Dixon's village, we continued on foot towards the hill and, linking up with the old Rafutho path, began slowly climbing into the slopes. High above, to the left of us, we caught sight of the topmost part of the Khubelu pass – two gigantic shoulders of blistered rock etched against the azure of a cloudless sky. Suddenly the path turned upwards through a disarray of boulders, ledges, shrivelled scrub and thornbush weighted with dust. In parts it was peppered with pebbles and cobbles, which made it slippery and hard on the ankles.

Halfway up the slope we came upon the first of a profusion of stone barricades and ramparts built by the Basotho during their occupation of Thaba Bosiu. A little farther, the path now veering to the right, we dragged ourselves on to a narrow terrace that linked up with the Khubelu pass. Above us towered the two shoulders of rock, the edges lined with several more ramparts and piles of stones. It was there that a dramatic event had taken place in the time of Moshesh that brought sorrow to the Boers of the neighbouring Orange Free State and jubilation to the inhabitants of Thaba Bosiu.

The Khubelu Pass

It was the year 1865. On 15 July a Boer army headed by General Jan Fick had bivouacked at Ha Rafutho, the blacksmith's village below the hill. The Boers had planned to take Thaba Bosiu, and subjugate Moshesh and his people with whom they had been in conflict for many years. So a little before noon, a party of some three hundred burghers, under Comdt Louw Wepener, crept up the slope towards the Khubelu pass, watched by hundreds of Basotho from behind the ramparts and barricades. They climbed unchallenged to the bottom of the 'gutter' (the fissure formed by the two shoulders of rock), but they were suddenly blasted with gunfire and then driven back by hundreds of boulders that came thundering upon them down the pass.

Wepener, accompanied by a coloured after-rider, had taken shelter among the rocks. But the moment the firing and boulder bombardment ceased, they again crawled cautiously up the pass. Wepener reached the terrace, climbed on to it and was instantly shot by the Basotho, who had been studying every move he had made. Then the defenders of the hill caught sight of his after-rider. He had also climbed on to the terrace and, kneeling beside his master's corpse was about to lift it, presumably to take it down the pass. Cheering wildly, the Basotho sent an avalanche of boulders over the top of the pass and on to the terrace. In a flash both Louw Wepener and his after-rider lay buried beneath its roaring mass.

This was to be the turning point in the Boers' assault on Thaba Bosiu; a second attack launched soon afterwards failed as dismally as the first. It was a battle that neither the invaders nor the Basotho would soon forget.

The distance from the terrace to the highest point of the Khubelu pass is no more than twenty metres, yet it took Khetheng and me almost as long to cover as the first stage of the climb up the Rafutho path. This was due partly to a procession of rocks that impeded our progress, partly to the steepness of the slope and partly to old Khetheng's legs, which seemed suddenly to become insubordinate. When at length we reached the crest of the pass, we found it matted with burrs and barricaded with bushes of prickly pear. Khetheng now paused to retrieve his breath and wipe the sweat from his face and neck. Leaning heavily on his stick, he eased himself to the ground. He then rolled on to his side and, covering his face with a handkerchief, sank quickly into a snory sleep.

Khetheng woke up ten minutes later and, rising to his feet, struck out along the track that led to Moshesh's village. I followed close on his heels, instinctively counting my strides to measure the distance between the top of the pass and the edge of the settlement. After exactly 284 paces we came suddenly upon three big boulders positioned in line across our path. Two of these, according to Khetheng, had been planted there in the time of Moshesh, and the third one after his death. They had once fronted the main entrance to Moshesh's old village, marking the spot where strangers were halted and questioned by guards. No one had ever dared to venture beyond them unless given permission by the chief himself. Close by was a cairn on which each visitor had been required to drop a stone, out of deference for the chief, before entering the village.

I had just inspected the cairn when, turning round, I beheld old Khetheng kneeling in prayer beside the middle boulder. Hands clasped tightly together, his face tilted skywards, he loudly directed his words to 'the great ancestor, Moshesh'. 'We crave your permission to enter the sacred village,' he quavered, 'and a blessing that will bring us happiness.'

As he continued to pray, his voice grew progressively softer, eventually fading into a whisper and then finally into unintelligible puffs of breath. Then, crying 'Amen', he rose and said exultantly: 'Our father is with us right now, and will remain with us not only today, but in all the days ahead until we die. Our father, Moshesh...we must be thankful to him for everything!'

The ruins of Moshesh's old village were clearly visible from where we stood beside the line of boulders. The nearest structure had once been a cylindrical, stone-wall hut, not unlike those I had seen on Butha-Buthe hill.

According to pioneer missionaries and visitors to Thaba Bosiu in the 1830s, the village was originally built in traditional style. James Backhouse, a traveller and friend of Moshesh, described the huts on the hill as 'universally of grass, and in the form of something like sparrow-pots'. The entrances, he noticed, were 'about a foot and a half high and wide and...arched with clay'. All the huts faced into 'circular courts' which were neatly plastered and enclosed with 'high reed-fencing'. Homes built of stone were a later feature of the settlement and had replaced most of the grass huts by 1839. They were erected by two adventurers from the Cape, Webster and Murphy, in return for forty oxen.

The two shoulders of rock that tower over the
Khubelu pass

Near the top of the Khubelu pass. Rafutho points
to the ramparts built during Moshesh's time

Part of the ruins of
Moshesh's village on Thaba
Bosiu

The Big Stone House

A short distance to the immediate right of the three boulders, Khetheng and I found the site of the largest of Moshesh's stone structures, the rectangular thatch-roofed house which had once been a source of great pride to him. Covered in grass and weeds, nothing but the faintest trace of its foundations remained, with the result that we found great difficulty in deciding exactly how big it had been. Having paced back and forth a number of times, we came to the conclusion it was roughly thirty metres long and twenty wide. It had consisted of a living room and a bedroom which, in the words of old Khetheng, were like 'two very big huts joined together, and covered by a single thatched roof, the biggest the Basotho had ever seen'.

This home, known to the Basotho as the Big Stone House, had been a conspicuous target for the Boers to blast with their cannons in 1865. It had been continuously bombarded during their assault on the Khubelu pass, and after the killing of Louw Wepener and his after-rider was finally razed to the ground.

Leaving the site of the Big Stone House, Khetheng and I continued along the track towards the ruins of Moshesh's village. As one by one the roofless walls of the huts came into view, I saw in my mind's eye scenes recorded in the diary of Eugene Casalis after a visit he had made to the settlement in 1833.

I could see the young Frenchman entering the village at the side of Letsie, Moshesh's eldest son, his face beaming with joy as hundreds of Basotho came surging forward to greet him and to sing songs in his honour. Reaching the huts, he was met by a party of dancing warriors, all of them bare-chested and dressed in loin skins. At the head of the dancers was a praise-singer named Rasebela. Said to be the shortest man in the village, he wore a skin mantle elaborately festooned with feathers, oxtails and tufts of fur. Rasebela was also an acrobat who could stand on his head and do cartwheels and somersaults without apparently ever tiring.

When Moshesh appeared and strode forward to welcome Casalis, the little praise-singer, much to the amusement of everyone present, began yelping like a dog, and then flung

left Ndundza maiden,
Roossenekal

right Ndundza diviner of
Tonteldoos dancing to the beat
of a tambourine

himself into a frenzied dance. Later, raising his voice for all to hear, he called upon the ancestors to watch over Moshesh, to protect him against evil and to bless his life with unending good fortune.

Greeting Casalis, Moshesh took him on a leisurely walk through the village. Rasebela followed them everywhere, and in order to attract their attention would caper around them in the guise of a monkey. As the missionary accompanied the chief, passing from one hut to another, his ears were filled with the adulations of the crowd, the bellowing of cattle and the barking of dogs. Soon they reached the *kgotla* (tribal court), a wide clearing with a spreading tree at the farthest side. Adjoining the *kgotla* was Moshesh's circular cattlefold which, Casalis noted, had been skilfully built of stones. Near by was the hut of Mamohato, the chief's senior wife. It was situated in the centre of a palisaded yard, and was part of a cluster of smaller huts that belonged to Moshesh's other wives.

The Frenchman had paused to exchange a few words with Queen Mamohato, and concluded she was a woman of outstanding calibre. In the years ahead he was to cherish her friendship and hospitality. When she died in 1854, he was in attendance at her funeral, helping to lay her to rest in a grave beneath the wall of Moshesh's cattlefold.

The visions of Casalis's visit to the once flourishing village began to fade from my mind, and were replaced by the stark reality of tumbledown huts choked with rubble, grass and burrs, and occupied by field mice, geckos and lizards. Standing among the ruins, I could see the spreading tree where the *kgotla* had been and a grassy mound which had served as a platform for Moshesh when he addressed his subjects on important occasions.

'That was a very important part of the village,' said old Khetheng pointing to the mound, 'for it was used not only by our father, Moshesh, but also by the councillors when they had announcements to make. And at nights it was used by old Akhosi.'

'Akhosi?' I queried.

'He was a watchman,' explained Khetheng, 'one of Moshesh's most faithful servants. Night after night he would sit on that mound and keep guard over the sleeping chief, his wives and children. Every now and then he would call out "hé-hé! hé-hé!", which was his way of signifying that all was well.'

Moshesh's Last Home

Of all the structures around us, the one that interested me most was a poky, two-roomed, rectangular home which, apart from the absence of a roof, was still in relatively good repair. This was where Moshesh had spent his declining years after the Big Stone House was destroyed by the Boers.

In August 1865, since their attempts to scale the Khubelu and other passes had failed, the Boers decided to build a chain of small but well fortified laagers around the base of the hill. In this way they could sever Moshesh's supply of food from the lowlands, and continue to pound his village with cannon fire.

Some two weeks before Comdt Wepener's hapless assault on the Khubelu defences, Moshesh had had some 15,000 cattle brought on to the hilltop, lest they fall into Boer hands. This decision, taken in haste, was to prove disastrous. There was barely grazing for 500 beasts on the summit, let alone thirty times as many.

Meanwhile Moshesh had taken shelter first in a shepherd's hut and then later in a cave tucked away in the western cliffs of Thaba Bosiu. By mid-September, the cattle had become frantic with hunger and thirst. Then one day, presumably catching the scent of water on a breeze that swept over the hill from the Phuthiatsana river, they began careering helter-skelter across the summit. Bedevilled, they burst through the village, scattering the inhabitants, capsizing the granaries and treading fowls, goats and sheep underfoot.

The spearhead of the stampede, finding itself swiftly approaching the eastern edge of the summit, split sharply to the left and right and then scattered in the direction of the Khubelu pass. In spite of this, fully a hundred beasts, propelled by the force of colliding bodies, went hurtling over the precipice and crashed to their deaths down the slopes of the hill. Soon great circles of vultures floated in from the highlands, skidded down to the carcasses and began to feast.

'Those were terrible times,' said Khetheng, 'not that I can remember; it was my grandfather who told me so. The whole of Thaba Bosiu suffered from the stink of rotting meat, and at nights no one could sleep because of the hyenas and jackals that fought with each other, howling and grunting among the carcasses. Then eventually the cattle on the hilltop began to die, and the stink became worse. There were vultures everywhere, some so heavy-bellied from overeating they were unable to fly. After dark, hyenas and jackals would climb up the passes and fight with each other over the meat. How could anyone sleep? It was an impossibility.

'It was only after Moshesh had decided to send most of the cattle back to the lowlands for the Boers to capture that things improved on the hill. What else could he do? Of course he had the carcasses buried, and in a very short time the hyenas and jackals returned to their hunting places along the river. So eventually a welcome stillness returned to Thaba Bosiu, although only at nights,' concluded Khetheng. 'During the daylight hours, there was often the roar of cannon fire, because unlike the vultures, hyenas and jackals, the Boers refused to move away.'

The blockade of Thaba Bosiu lasted for over three years. Soon after the loss of his cattle, Moshesh sent an envoy to Sir Philip Wodehouse, then the High Commissioner at the Cape, with a plea for the British to annex Lesotho. But to his consternation, Moshesh found Sir Philip unsympathetic and unwilling to involve his government in a dispute with the Boers. Moshesh was bewildered. His people were hungry and broken in spirit. In the lowlands some of his vassal chiefs had forsaken the struggle, and even his most redoubtable military commanders talked of surrender. His councillors had started to quarrel with one another and to embark on intrigues and duplicities. At the beginning of 1868 he became ill. He was confined to the very stone-house that Khetheng and I had now come to see.

During the following ten months, the old chief groused and fretted and delighted in talking about his impending death. Then came gladdening news from Wodehouse; the British government had agreed to annex Lesotho. Moshesh could look forward to a new era of peace. Sir Philip Wodehouse journeyed from the Cape to Thaba Bosiu in February 1869 and, escorted to Moshesh's little stone house, found him asleep beneath a pile of blankets and skins. The interior of this modest home was drab and impoverished. It was dark and stuffy and furnished with damaged chairs, a rickety table, a shabby sofa draped in leopard skins and a mat of eland hide positioned in the centre of a worn clay floor. It was a far cry from the comparatively luxurious Big Stone House of former years, and reflected the level to which Moshesh, a man of great dignity, had been reduced as a result of the war. He was, nevertheless, to find this modest home more than adequate for his historical meeting with Philip Wodehouse. Indeed within its dingy walls a bond of

Khetheng at the doorway of the home where Moshesh spent his declining years

friendship between Lesotho and Britain was sealed forever. And Moshesh's most cherished dream had come true.

When I entered Moshesh's tiny bedroom with Khetheng I thought of the anguish the old chief suffered in the months after Wodehouse's visit to Thaba Bosiu. His health had quickly deteriorated and, although peace had returned to Thaba Bosiu – the Boers having withdrawn after Wodehouse's visit – he was beset by anxieties.

During the winter of 1869 he contracted both influenza and a stomach disorder and came close to death, which left him frail and unable to walk without the aid of attendants. By the end of the year he was virtually bedridden and, sensing the approach of death, became apprehensive of what lay in store for him in the life to come. Over the past thirty-seven years he had adamantly refused conversion to Christianity. Now under pressure from the missionaries he suddenly changed his mind.

At the end of February 1870, Moshesh openly declared Jesus Christ as his Father and Saviour, and arranged with the missionaries to be baptized on 12 March. He sent messengers throughout Lesotho and beyond its borders with news of his decision, and a request that his subjects and friends should attend the ceremony. He had the interior of the stone house plastered and painted white, and a lofty, soil platform built on the outskirts of the village. This was where he wished to be baptized. He was determined that the proceedings should be clearly seen.

By the tenth of the month, Thaba Bosiu swarmed with thousands of people – Basotho chiefs, councillors, warriors and commoners, emissaries from neighbouring tribal territories and a handful of missionaries. There was even a British envoy in the village who, unaware of the celebration, had arrived with a message for Moshesh: Queen Victoria had gratefully accepted a leopard-skin *kaross* sent to her by the old chief some months before.

But Moshesh slept peacefully through all the excitement. Waking hazily at daybreak on the morning of 11 March, he exchanged a few words with his son, Letsie. He then closed his eyes and floated silently away to join his ancestors in the realm of spirits.

The Burial Grounds

Khetheng and I spent almost an hour among the ruins of Moshesh's home, taking measurements of its two tiny rooms, and rummaging through the debris that coated the floor.

Among a pile in the old chief's living room, we found fragments of nineteenth-century floral crockery and chips of dark blue glass, which we concluded were the remains of old medicine bottles. We also discovered a rusty assegai blade, two lead bullets and a grinding stone. Our next discovery was a little frightening: the stones at the bottom of the pile swarmed with scorpions. Suddenly exposed to sunlight, they went skittering across our feet, nippers outstretched and tails arched in readiness to sting. This brought our investigations abruptly to a close, and we moved on towards the southern extremity of the summit, bound for the burial grounds of Thaba Bosiu.

Outside the ruins of Moshesh's village we followed a path through a thicket of aloes, and entered a stretch of sand dunes as bleak and lifeless as would be found in any southern African desert. We had barely crossed this powdery waste when we came upon a patch of finely-chipped stones. Here I picked up a number of Stone Age artifacts – arrowheads, spearheads, scrapers, awls and drills. It was a find that prodded my imagination, for now I realized that not only the Basotho but also peoples of bygone centuries had used the summit of Thaba Bosiu as a place of refuge.

Moving on to the burial grounds we located Moshesh's grave. This, in the words of Khetheng, was the most holy place in the whole of Lesotho.

'In these burial grounds,' he said, in a sepulchral tone, 'our father sleeps, and around him in all those other graves, not only his sons and their sons who ruled after him, but other great chiefs of the nation.'

I reflected on Moshesh's burial service. It had been conducted by the Revd Jousse, who had arrived at Thaba Bosiu in 1855 after the recall of Eugene Casalis to France. The proceedings had been lengthy, and a tiring experience for the thousands of mourners. Apart from the prayers and sermon delivered by the missionary, and dirges sung by the late chief's subjects, a number of Basotho dignitaries took turns in extolling the virtues of their departed leader. And while the grave was being filled, and a cairn built over it, the crowd pressed together filling the air with lamentations. Finally Letsie placed a rectangular stone at the head of the grave, a slab of shale into which was chipped the name most ardently revered in all the Lesotho – MOSHESH.

Standing beside Moshesh's grave with Khetheng, I noticed he was deeply moved and on the brink of tears. I was about to take a photograph of the burial grounds when he raised a hand in protest, explaining we had first to pay our respects to the nation's father. He then removed his hat and, sinking to his knees, began to pray. He thanked Moshesh for many things, and most particularly for the health that he, Clark Khetheng, had always enjoyed. Even now in old age he was healthy and happy, and although resigned to the fact that his time for dying was fast approaching, he could genuinely say he had no cause to fret. He was not afraid to die. However, in anticipation of the event, he had an important request to make: he wanted to be laid to rest on Thaba Bosiu, the hill he had always loved so much. It was his fervent wish to be buried as close as possible to Moshesh's grave.

When he had finished praying and I had taken a photograph of the burial grounds, Khetheng drew my attention to the disrepair and untidy condition of Moshesh's grave. 'I can't understand why this should be,' he said angrily, 'especially as our people come regularly here to pray, and even more especially when you consider that year after year, on 12 March (which is the day our father, Moshesh, is honoured by the nation) Basotho pilgrims come to this holy place, hundreds of them at a time, including their headmen and chiefs. Many a time I have been tempted to rebuild it myself, but I'm afraid to start. Afraid I'll be accused of meddling with matters that don't really concern me.'

The old man gazed pensively at the grave, chin in hand. 'I've a plan,' he said, raising a finger in a gesture of triumph, 'I'll speak to Dixon Rafutho. Perhaps he as a councillor and descendant of Rafutho, the blacksmith, can persuade our chief to do something about this.

'Now I feel better,' he smiled, 'so let us move on.'

Khetheng led me through the burial grounds, pausing to point out the graves of paramount chiefs who had ruled after Moshesh – Letsie I who died in 1891, Lerotholi in 1905, Letsie II in 1913 and Griffith in 1939.

'If only you could have seen some of those funerals, as I saw them,' Khetheng reminisced as we left the burial grounds and started retracing our steps towards the Khubelu pass.

'It was always our custom,' he continued, 'for commoners to be buried in the floor of their huts, babies in ash heaps and chiefs in the cattlefold. But burial up here, on Thaba Bosiu, could be very different, especially if the one to be buried was a ruler who had lived in the lowlands. Then his corpse was carried to the foot of the hill, near Rafutho's village, and passed by hundreds of men, standing shoulder to shoulder, up the Khubelu pass and across the hilltop until it reached the grave. During its slow and difficult journey, the royal corpse

Bushman paintings in a cave below the southern precipices of Thaba Bosiu

was never allowed to touch the ground until, of course, it was lowered into the hole where it would rest forever. That was something to see!'

It was almost sunset when Khetheng and I arrived back at my truck, on the outskirts of Dixon Rafutho's village. Dixon, who had been in Maseru all day and had just returned home, came out to greet us. He expressed deep regret at having missed us, especially as he had not been up the hill for some considerable time and would greatly have enjoyed the outing.

'Will you be coming again?' he asked me.

'Yes,' I nodded, 'for sure I will.'

'Then you must let me know well before the time,' he said, 'because Khetheng is no longer young and strong, and I believe it's right I should be with him.'

They left me now and headed for Dixon's village. I spent the night in Maseru, and set out next morning for home.

Four years were to pass before I returned to Lesotho. This time I arrived at the beginning of September and spent the first two weeks researching in Butha-Buthe, Mamathe, Matsieng and in the districts of Peka, Mafeteng and Quthing.

The burial grounds of Basotho chiefs on Thaba
Bosiu

Royal village, Matsieng

A young mother, Matsieng royal village

Tseliso Khamelo of
Thaba Bosiu, one
of Khetheng's oldest
friends

The author and Rafutho (with stick) at
Khetheng's grave
(Photo: Alpheus Hlatshwayo)

During the third week I called on Dixon Rafutho at Thaba Bosiu, hoping he and Khetheng would accompany me up the hill. But on meeting Dixon, I discovered that Khetheng had died not long after my previous visit. He, Dixon, offered to act as my guide in place of our departed friend and also suggested we visit old Khetheng's grave.

So Dixon and I climbed the Khubelu pass together during the early afternoon, inspected the ramparts, the old village and other sites I had previously seen, and then headed for the burial grounds. Reaching Moshesh's grave, we shared a minute or two of silence beside it. My mind flashed back to the day I had stood at this holy place with old Khetheng. The grave had looked neglected then, but now it was infinitely worse. I wondered what the old man would have said had he been with us now.

Moving on towards the edge of the burial grounds, we came to a modest mound overgrown with grass. This was where Clark Khetheng had been lain to rest.

Moshesh had heard his prayer.

My next visit to Lesotho was in May 1965. After three weeks of research among villages and cattleposts in the highlands, I again went to Dixon's home, only to find he had just left for Leribe, and would not be returning before three or four days.

A little downcast, I set out for the mission station in search of someone to accompany me to the burial grounds. At the mission church I came upon an elderly man called Tseliso Khamelo and his son, Albert, reclining in the shade of the syringa tree. Learning that Dixon was away in Leribe, they volunteered to take his place as my guides. According to Tseliso, he and Khetheng had been friends since childhood and had often gone together to the summit.

So Tseliso, Albert and I departed immediately for the Khubelu pass, and reached the burial grounds an hour later. I was amazed to find that Moshesh's grave had changed. The cairn had been rebuilt, every trace of the grass and weeds removed and the headstone replaced by a taller one. It in no way resembled the grave I had known in years gone by.

'Don't you think our holy place looks better now?' asked Tseliso with a smile.

'Very much better,' I replied.

'And I'm sure the one most pleased is our late brother, Khetheng,' he added.

'You're right,' I nodded, 'so very right.'

Moshesh's grave

Ndebele

When I look back on the many years I have devoted to field research among the indigenous peoples of southern Africa, I believe this would never have come about had I not been born and raised in a rural environment.

Like Stevenson's young Jim Hawkins, whose affection was captured and imagination awakened by a patch-eyed pirate, I too had a boyhood hero – an elderly Ndebele patriarch named Sipho Mncube. Born in the present-day Roossenekal district in the early 1870s, Sipho had moved westwards at the age of thirty and settled among a small group of Ndebele south of Pretoria. He was accompanied by his wife Malunka, their five-year-old daughter, a dog, a cow and some goats.

In 1923 he arrived at Veld View, my parents' farm in Rivonia, where he was engaged by my father as a foreman. By this time, he and Malunka had had three more children, all of them boys, the youngest of which was an infant in arms. I myself was a baby at the time, so my earliest recollections of Sipho date back to roughly 1926.

There were three other Ndebele families living and working on Veld View at the time of Sipho's arrival. The men and youths were employed as farmhands, the women as domestic servants, hoers, reapers or fruit-pickers and the male children as herdboys. Sipho was their adviser and spokesman. He was known to them all as *uBaba* – Father. He was a tall, lean and angular man, with large, nodular hands and feet and a shock of greying hair. Squint-eyed and bearded, he had irregular, tobacco-stained teeth, gaping nostrils and ears that stood out sideways.

He was far from handsome, this hero of mine, not that I noticed then or even cared. As a little farm boy, I saw him in a different light, and could recognize only his more attractive qualities – his genial disposition, his sparkling wit, his love for laughter and, above all, his extraordinary gift for storytelling. Indeed, Sipho Mncube was unrivalled in Rivonia as a narrator of African folktales and history, and his ghost stories could chill even the boldest among us. Since those far-off times, I have enjoyed the company of hundreds of narrators in all parts of southern Africa, and have yet to find his equal.

As both my parents were middle-aged at the time of my birth – Sipho used to delight in referring to my untimely arrival as a late lambing in the season – and because my two brothers were considerably older than I, my age-mates were predominantly African herdboys. By sharing their company from day to day, I learned to speak Sindebele (a dialect of Zulu) at an early age, as well as more than a smattering of Southern Sotho which was widely spoken in Rivonia.

Thabo, Sipho's youngest son, was my closest companion. He and I, with other age-mates, spent much of our spare time either near the Jukskei river, where the cattle were grazed and watered, or at the cluster of huts above the farmhouse where the African workers and their families lived.

As a storyteller, old Sipho was at his best after dark when the day's work was done, the evening meal over and he had downed a few ladles of sorghum beer. On most nights when I was able to slip away from the farmhouse and visit his huts, I would find him seated with a handful of cronies in a circle around an outdoor fire. Invariably they would be exchanging anecdotes, bandying tales about ghosts, ghouls and earth-bound spirits or recounting the lives of historical African personages such as King Shaka and his assassin, Dingane; the renegade chiefs, Matiwane and Mpangazitha, Queen Mantatisi and her Wild Cat army and, of course, the great Moshesh. His favourite character was the Matabele conqueror, Mzilikazi. When he, Mzilikazi, fled from Shaka he moved not westwards, as the two other Zulu chiefs had done, but northwards, and therefore beyond reach of *Difaqane*.

'Mzilikazi was the greatest of them all, even greater than Shaka!' old Sipho would bellow, his cronies fervently agreeing with him, and the children with whom I sat snuggled in the shadows nodding their heads approvingly.

Of all his stories, the most exciting were those that dealt with the escapades of Mzilikazi. Yet in later life, long after Sipho had left Rivonia (his health failing and his mind set on returning to his birthplace), it was not the stories he had told us about Mzilikazi or Shaka or Moshesh I remembered best, but episodes he had gleaned from the history of his very own people, the Ndebele. Just as impressive were his descriptions of Ndebele culture as he knew it in early manhood. This explains why I chose this tribe, old Sipho's people, for my very first venture into field research in 1946.

Chief uMusi

Although they are the smallest tribal group in southern Africa, the Ndebele are widely known, even in the remotest parts, for their outstanding craftsmanship, their beautiful homes and villages and their distinctive and highly colourful mode of dress and ornamentation. Closely linked in origin with the Zulu, they inhabited part of KwaZulu until two centuries before King Shaka's rise to power. Then, presumably as the result of factional feuding, they migrated inland, eventually establishing themselves on the plains and in the bush-clad hills just north of where Pretoria stands today. Their chief at the time is said to have been uMusi, a wily ruler whose first concern had always been to protect his subjects against exploitation by other more powerful tribes. uMusi was not a fighting man, nor had the Ndebele ever been a belligerent tribe.

According to old Sipho and Ndebele chroniclers I was to meet in later years, Chief uMusi had six wives and at least thirty children, the most important of which were six strapping sons born to the *indlunkulu*, his senior queen. He was a just and respected ruler, whose gentle disposition was to earn him the confidence of the Sotho tribes among whom he and his people had settled. Soon the Ndebele started building villages, tilling new lands and planting crops. During the following twenty years, they lived in peace, becoming increasingly prosperous.

Then, suddenly, uMusi died and Manala, his eldest son, was named as the future chief of the tribe. The announcement was immediately challenged by Ndundza, another of the senior sons. Before long, the two brothers faced each other like angry bulls vying for supremacy over a herd. As they squabbled and hurled threats at each other, the rest of the tribe, choosing sides, split the Ndebele into opposing factions. Neither would yield and Manala, Ndundza and their followers prepared for battle.

In a bloody struggle near the late chief's village, Ndundza was defeated and put to flight. So, gathering as many of the tribe as were prepared to accompany him, he headed eastwards, eventually finding a place to settle along the upper reaches of the Olifants river. Meanwhile, amidst great celebration, the victorious Manala was installed as chief over his father's domain. But no sooner had he moved into his new royal village than two additional factions, headed by the new chief's remaining brothers, broke away from the tribe. The Kekana section moved northwards and settled in the region of Zebedelia and the other, under its leader, Dlomo, returned to the east coast whence the Ndebele had originally come.

By the middle of the nineteenth century, the Ndebele in the north had further divided into splinter groups, occupying patches of territory around Zebedelia, Potgietersrust and Pietersburg. As a result of their close association with the more powerful Sotho-speaking tribes of those parts, they had gradually forsaken their mother tongue for the Sotho language, and had also undergone considerable cultural change. By contrast the descendants of Manala and Ndundza had retained much of their original cultural identity. Linguistically they had hardly changed since the days of their illustrious ancestor, Chief uMusi.

During the 1850s the Ndundza faction, then ruled by a chief named Mabogo, was faced with a frightening situation: the Transvaal was being gradually infiltrated by Boers in search of a northern hinterland. The White men were known to have built towns and established farms between the Olifants and Steelpoort rivers, and were considered by the Ndundza as impostors and a threat to peace. It was rumoured the Boers had entered into land agreements with the powerful neighbouring Pedi tribes, and Mabogo conferred with his councillors with a view to discussing what action, if any, was necessary. After lengthy debate, it was decided that, as a token of friendship, the chief should send gifts of cattle and grain to the farmers' newly-founded headquarters in Lydenburg. By winning their confidence in this way, it was felt the Ndundza could look to the Boers for help in times of need. At all costs they were never to be antagonized.

During the following eighteen months, despite efforts by the Ndundza to befriend the Boers, the relationship between them deteriorated. The reason was that, contrary to Mabogo's orders, some of his subjects had begun lifting cattle from nearby farms. By the autumn of 1864 stock theft had become so rife that the Boers had started mustering their commandos for a punitive expedition into Ndundza territory. They were actually on the verge of setting out for Mabogo's village, when they learned the Ndundza had been attacked and decimated by Swazi marauders. Later they discovered the survivors had settled in scattered groups around Belfast, Bethal, Bronkhorstspruit and Middelburg. The commandos were disbanded. The Ndundza, the Boers concluded, had ceased to exist as a united tribe.

Roossenekal

During the following decade, many of the Ndundza, plagued by unyielding impoverishment, ventured back to the north and sought sanctuary among the Pedi and other tribes. Some of them even found their way on to Boer farms, and became employed as herdsmen and labourers. But the year 1870 heralded a more promising era for the diehards of the tribe who had remained behind, bringing forth a new and ambitious young chief called Nyabela in place of Mabogo. Among Nyabela's foremost aims was the reunification of the scattered tribe. As a first step he established headquarters in the most rugged section of the Steenkamp mountains, overlooking the Steelpoort river and the present-day town of Roossenekal. By 1882, Nyabela's humble headquarters had grown into an elaborately fortified settlement inhabited by some 8,000 of his subjects. Not a year later it lay in ruins, stripped of its people, its granaries and stock by the horrors of war.

'My heart never ceased to ache,' I can hear old Sipho say as if it were yesterday, 'because that was where I lived with my parents, my relatives and very many friends, all of us knowing the joy of living. Ah yes, in the time of Chief Nyabela it was like knowing you belonged to some kind of heaven, and then suddenly seeing it turn into hell.'

I climbed the Steenkamp mountains to Nyabela's old settlement in 1946, then nine years later and again in February 1976. During my first visit, I travelled by train to Dullstroom, and walked twenty kilometres across the hills to Tonteldoos, a farming district with a solitary trading store. There I borrowed a horse from a farmer called Boom Joubert, and struck out westwards for Roossenekal.

For three days I travelled a dusty road through sprawling valleys, hillslopes lush with bush, tree-aloes and thatching grass and plains threaded with rivulets. Along the way, I called in at farmhouses and Ndebele homesteads, continually questioning people whose forebears had lived in the time of Chief Nyabela. In this way I gathered a wealth of information about the events that led to the destruction of the Ndundza tribe in 1883.

Nyabela, I learned, had been a peace-loving chief, revered by his subjects and respected by most of the Boers in neighbouring areas. The site he had selected twelve years before for the resettlement of his people was about halfway up the southern slopes of the Steenkamp range. His personal home had been at the foot of an agglomeration of cliffs, boulders and indigenous trees, and within easy reach of a network of underground caves. Hundreds of other homes were grouped on terraces to the left and right of the cliffs. They were intertwined with innumerable stone walls, some serving as courtyard enclosures and others as loop-holed parapets. By 1882, Nyabela and his subjects had come to believe their settlement was impregnable. Apart from the

Ndundza homestead. An ox-skull fixed to the top
of the pole serves to frighten hawks from the
family's chickens

difficult terrain that embraced it and its multiplicity of walls
and parapets, it was manned by a small but efficient fighting
force, part of which was armed with javelins and the rest with
contraband firearms supplied to the chief by White itinerant
traders.

In August 1882 Nyabela, now in the prime of his
chieftaincy, unwittingly placed himself in a situation that
would lead to his downfall. He gave sanctuary to a fugitive
chief named Mampuru who, in plotting to usurp the throne
of the Pedi tribes, had murdered its paramount chief,
Sekhukhune I. Nyabela refused to surrender Mampuru to the
Boers. This led to bitter dissension, and by the end of
September there was talk of war. Two months later, Nyabela
received news that a commando of two thousand Boers,

supported by a large contingent of Pedi warriors, had been
spotted by Ndundza scouts in the west. The chief is said to
have considered handing Mampuru over to the Boers, in a
bid to prevent possible bloodshed. He is also said to have
considered fleeing northwards but, assured by his military
commanders that the Boers could be vanquished, he gave
orders for the Ndundza to prepare for war. The commando
arrived soon afterwards.

As the following nine months were to reveal, the Boers,
under command of Comdt General Piet Joubert, found the
Ndundza an elusive foe, and virtually impossible to engage in
battle. Looking up from the valleys into the Steenkamp
range, all they could see was a vast expanse of thornbush,
euphorbia and umbrella-shaped trees, the tips of cliffs and

smoke from the hearths of indiscernible huts. When their reconnoitring parties ventured into the slopes, they were ambushed, stoned and shot at. The Ndundza were found to be not only elusive but also extremely aggressive.

Concerned at the hit and run tactics of Nyabela's snipers by day, and their incursions into the Boer encampments by night, Joubert had a chain of mud forts built along the base of the Steenkamp range. There was little action during December and the following two months, but in March 1882, during regular skirmishing along the lower slopes of the mountain, three Boers were killed and eleven wounded. These casualties came as a shock to Piet Joubert; he decided to blockade the settlement. Once the Ndundza were cut off from the surrounding valleys, their food supply would quickly diminish. This was what the Boers had done during the siege of Thaba Bosiu, Joubert reflected. Only the intervention of the British had saved Moshesh.

As soon as the blockade had been instituted, the Boers set fire to the slopes of the mountain, hoping the flames would drive the Ndundza into their hands. But these tactics produced no significant result. The Boers were dumbfounded, but not unduly discouraged. Having prevented the Ndundza from planting crops in spring, they knew that the settlement's grain supply would not last for long. They decided to harness their impatience, and wait for the autumn, even, if need be, the winter to pass.

In the meantime, a party of Boers was assigned to cutting a trench up the mountain slope, in the direction of Nyabela's settlement. The aim was to get as close to the caves as possible, then to dig a tunnel and seek an opening through which charges of dynamite could be fed. In the course of this daring operation, several burghers were killed by snipers, including two officers, Roos and Senekal. So, discontinuing the plan for a while, the Boers built an elongated metal fort on wheels, which they laboriously pushed up the trench. This gave them ample protection: they could continue the tunnel as originally planned.

The blockade was to take effect far sooner than the Boers had anticipated. The Ndundza had consumed the last of their grain in February, and had also cleared the trees of edible fruits, leaves and bark and the soil of bulbs, tubers and roots. In addition, every trace of game had disappeared from the

Entrance to the inner courtyard of an Ndundza homestead

mountain slopes as a result of incessant hunting and snaring. Even mice, lizards, hares, birds and insects were difficult to come by. In fact, food was so scarce that the few milch cows kept in the settlement had to be slaughtered. By May, the Ndundza resorted to meals prepared from grass and cowdung. Many were suffering from stomach and other disorders. All of them knew that sooner or later they would have to surrender or die.

At the beginning of June, a group of greybeards came down from the mountain and begged the Boers for food. Taken to Joubert, they described the plight of Nyabela's people, adding that many were angry with the chief for continuing to harbour Mampuru, the murderer. Loyalties were divided, they said, and the Ndundza were on the brink of surrender.

Encouraged by this news, the Boers decided to launch a full-scale attack on the settlement. They were, however, ambushed, pelted with stones, peppered with gun-slug and bombarded with boulders. Retreating swiftly, they managed to escape with surprisingly few casualties. Nyabela, they told each other, was as sly as a jackal. They would not allow themselves to be tricked again.

The blockade continued, and during the following ten days the fighting amounted to no more than sporadic exchanges of gunfire. July arrived, ushering in the most austere and gloomy midwinter the Ndundza had ever known. They were starving now, and could speak of nothing but the agonizing prospect of death. Then one morning the settlement began to erupt and quake, the caves to roll about and disintegrate. The Boers had completed the tunnel. The dynamite thundered incessantly. Stricken with terror, the women and children and most of the men came struggling down the paths to the valleys, a wailing, whimpering throng crying out for mercy. They were followed by a councillor bearing a flag of truce, and a messenger with news that Nyabela had decided to surrender. Chief Mampuru had gone into hiding among caves near the confluence of the Klip and Steelpoort rivers, the messenger added. He would be captured and delivered to the Boers by Nyabela himself.

On 7 July, Mampuru was handed over to the Boers, and four days later Nyabela arrived in camp. Like his captive, Nyabela was taken into custody and sent to Pretoria to stand trial before a judge and jury.

Before breaking camp and returning to their homes, the Boers set fire first to Nyabela's royal village and then to the rest of the settlement in the Steenkamp range. The Ndundza

An Ndundza diviner (left) and her client

Ndundza maiden

dispersed and fled to the highveld plains in the south, where they had lived for a short while after the Swazi invasion in 1864. Some of them found sanctuary in the villages of kinsmen and Pedi chiefs, but by far the majority drifted into White areas, and offered their services to the Boers as farm labourers.

On 22 November 1883, Mampuru was found guilty for the murder of Chief Sekhukhune and hanged in Pretoria. For his part in the episode, Nyabela was sentenced to fifteen years' imprisonment. Thus ended a second tragic era in the history of a tiny section of a tiny tribe. Today the Ndebele of the Eastern Transvaal speak with reverence of Nyabela's settlement in the Steenkamp mountains. Just as Sipho Mncube once described it to me, as a beautiful place, a part of heaven that turned into hell.

An Inhospitable Settlement

When I visited what remained of Nyabela's settlement in 1946 I had hoped to locate old Sipho and his family in Roossenekal. I spent the first day calling on farmers along the Steelpoort river, believing their Ndebele servants might know of his whereabouts, but I could find no one who had ever heard of him. However one morning, when I had already abandoned the search, I met an old man near the river who professed to remember Sipho.

'He is the one with a squint and the very brown teeth and the very great love for talking and talking,' the old man said. 'He came back to this district a few years ago, and because he was sickly lived with Mahlangu, his brother, not far from Roossenekal. Then one day Mahlangu moved away to Tafelkop near Groblersdal, taking Sipho and his family with him. By that time, your old friend was even sicker and weaker,' the old man concluded, 'so I believe that by now he must be dead.'

That was the last I was to hear of Sipho Mncube.

Compared to Moshesh's strongholds at Butha-Buthe and Thaba Bosiu, I found climbing the slopes to Nyabela's old settlement relatively easy. Apparently at the time of its occupation by the Ndundza, there were several paths leading to and from it. I could find only two – one on the southern slope of the mountain and another a short distance to the west. These meandered steeply upwards through groves of thorn trees, tree-aloes and euphorbia sprinkled with boulders and anthills. Here and there they cut through shoulder-high thatching grass, and in parts they were overgrown with stinging nettles, burrs and devil thorns.

Halfway up the southern path one enters a twisting avenue of indigenous trees – white stinkwood, buffalo thorn, olive and some of the biggest wild fig trees in all southern Africa. About a hundred paces from the start of the path, the first of the parapets comes into view, some curling upwards along the contours of the slopes, some jutting sideways and others cresting huge slabs of granite, or terraces once built by Nyabela's subjects. Now the path swerves sharply to the right, bringing into view a succession of walls, all neatly built of chiselled stones. These are punctuated with loopholes, most of them now blocked with moss and ferns. There are also the gaps of narrow gateways, indicating where the homesteads were situated in the time of Chief Nyabela.

Higher up the path snakes through a jumble of spherical boulders, moss-clad tree trunks and a chaos of undergrowth. It then enters a rambling clearing lined in the foreground with taller parapets and thick-stemmed ironwood trees and in the rear with cliffs. This is where Chief Nyabela had lived; this had been his personal retreat.

The opening to Nyabela's caves is to the left of the clearing in the shadow of the cliffs. As the custodian of the settlement, a patriarch named Pepetwana Skosana, pointed out to me, it resembles the mouth of a gigantic bullfrog, its lower jaw supporting a tongue of rounded rock, and its gullet receding into a string of hollows in the bowels of the earth.

Entering the caves, first treading cautiously across a narrow vestibule and then sliding downwards through moist and mossy passageways, one's nostrils revolt against the pungent stench of bat and rock-rabbit droppings and urine. Very soon, feeling disillusioned and, indeed, unwelcome in those murky depths, one yearns for a taste of fresh air. So, crawling back towards the mouth, amidst the squeaking of bats and the flurrying of their wings, one prods the inky surroundings with the beam of a torch and, suddenly remembering what Skosana, the custodian, had said about snakes that take shelter in this very same place, one shivers a little. But if you are as fortunate as I was in 1976 to stumble upon a rusty Ndebele spear blade, or a grinding stone or fragments of pottery, you are bound to forget about bats and snakes, and your nostrils no longer pick up the stench.

On each of my three visits to the old settlement, I took delight in climbing on to a massive boulder beside the caves, the granite 'throne' once used by Chief Nyabela. It was there

The terrain immediately below Nyabela's caves and 'gallows cliff'

One of many passages leading to subterranean
chambers in the bowels of the Steenkamp
mountains

that he presided over his tribal court, held meetings with
visiting dignitaries or addressed his councillors and army
commanders.

In 1946 I ventured to climb the tallest cliff in the
settlement, the so-called 'gallows cliff', where according to
Skosana, people found guilty of cowardice, treachery or
murder were put to death by the chief's executioners. Finding
it crowned with a colony of lizards, a bevy of iguana and a
solitary white-necked cobra, I quickly slid downwards,
dislodging a cascade of rubble and landing with a thud in a
cloud of dust.

Manala Village

Of the many Ndebele villages scattered over the Transvaal, the most elaborate and beautiful are found not among Chief Nyabela's descendants in the east, but among the Manala section of the tribe in regions to the north of Pretoria.

The largest of the Manala villages is serenely situated in the bushveld area near de Wildt. I visited it for the first time in 1953, and since then have continued to do so at regular intervals. The headman, Msiza II, was to become my mentor in various aspects of Ndebele culture. I spent many fruitful days in discussion with him, until his death in 1965.

In 1953 I arrived on the outskirts of Msiza's village on a sunny midwinter morning, and while I was parking my truck in the shade of a thorntree an elderly man came forward to greet me. Learning I wanted to meet the headman, he led me to a cattlefold where I found Msiza braying a goat-skin pegged to the ground. Short, lean and middle-aged, Msiza rose to his feet when he saw me approaching. He then shook me by the hand and suggested I sit down beside him while he continued to work.

During the following four hours, we discussed not only the Manala, but also the Ndebele of Roossenekal. He invited me to do field research among his own subjects and promised to introduce me to informants who knew just as much about Ndebele culture as he did. This I gladly accepted, agreeing to start on the following morning.

At that time, the huts of Msiza's village were rondavel-style – in more recent times rectangular homes have become the vogue – and they stood side by side, perfectly in line, from north to south. They were separated from each other by tall earthen walls, forming private courtyards, and were roofed with reeds and thatching grass. I was fortunate to arrive at the village as a new hut was about to be built, and was able to take note of each step in its construction from start to finish.

When a site has been selected for a new home, the Manala summon a medicine man whose function, among other things, is not only to solicit the blessing of the ancestors, but also to ensure that the future occupants will be protected against the insidious activities of sorcerers and other evil-doers.

Taking a sacrificial sheep provided for the occasion by the owner of the hut to be built, the medicine man daubs it with indigenous medicines and then cuts its throat with a single stroke of a razor-sharp knife. The moment the carcass has been skinned and cut open, he gathers the entrails, which he

deposits in the centre of the chosen site. Now he sprinkles the building materials – pegs, poles and thatching grass – with protective and purifying medicines. Then work begins amidst the hubbub of rejoicing spectators.

First a peg is driven into the ground, and tied with a piece of string about three metres long. Using a sharpened stick attached to the opposite end of the string, one of the workers traces the outline of the circular hut floor on to the ground. Other workers begin digging holes about an arm's length apart, following the outline. When the holes are ready, heavy poles, two and a half metres tall, are planted and carefully scrutinized to ensure they are parallel and also level on top. Then wooden wall-plates are secured to the top of the poles with nails. Now follows the arduous task of constructing a net-like frame for the walls, following the line of the upright poles. Made of saplings, the frame is compactly interwoven with pliable twigs. Three large spaces are left in the completed cylindrical framework – two windows and an east-facing doorway.

A striking feature of the Manala rondavel hut is an outer corridor which embraces about half of the structure, beginning at the doorway. This is built by a group of men as soon as the hut-frame is ready. It too is made with saplings and twigs, and it stands as tall as the inner walls.

Meanwhile a second party of men constructs a frame for the conical roof. The women fetch grass and prepare daub for the walls from clay and cowdung. A large group of elderly women, assisted by teenage girls, attends to the catering, regularly presenting the workers with platters of roasted goat meat, boiled chicken and cereals, or replenishing their drinking gourds with sorghum beer.

When the roof-frame is ready, it is laboriously lifted by a circle of men on to the cylindrical structure, the eaves extending far beyond the corridor. Once the frame is firmly fastened to the wall-plates, thatching begins; the men sit on top of the roof while the women keep them constantly supplied with sheaves of grass. Then a platoon of women, bearing daub in buckets or basins, apply it thickly on the inner and outer sides of the woven frame. This task may take two or three days to complete; the walls of a Manala hut are made broad and firm, and have to be carefully smoothed with the palm of the hand.

The courtyard is measured and its walls erected as soon as the hut is complete. Then its floor is laid and plastered with daub. A rectangular granary made of reeds is built at the rear of the hut, and beside it a modest shelter for storing sorghum beer, pumpkins, gourds, melons and maize on the cob. In due course, the courtyard will serve as the place where members of the family can sit leisurely together in the company of friends. The hut, on the other hand, will serve not only as sleeping quarters and as a shelter on cold or rainy days, but also as the place where relatives and friends can sit snugly together around an open hearth, especially on wintry nights.

A Manala hut is never cluttered with family belongings, and great pains are taken to keep it clean and neat. Indeed each morning when the sleepers rise, they move their blankets, sleeping mats, utensils, stools and clothing into the adjacent corridors, where foodstuffs and other household goods are stored.

Mural Decoration

At the time of their arrival in the interior of southern Africa, long before the rule of King Shaka, the Ndebele tribes lived in dome-shaped huts built entirely of timber and grass. That was the fashion among the east-coast peoples whence they had come. The change to a rondavel-style home is likely to have been a gradual process, brought about through contact with the Pedi and other inland tribes. This also applies to the gift the newcomers developed for mural decoration, a form of art in which the Manala in particular eventually learned to excel.

Mural decoration is the prerogative of women; the motifs, patterns and colours closely resemble those found in their beadwork. Manala walls carry a great variety of designs with the most elaborate and ornate on the outer surfaces of the courtyards, the façades and inner walls of huts. Patterns embrace a large number of shapes and symbols – squares, rectangles, circles, spheres and triangles; silhouetted flowers, birds, animals and snakes; letters of the alphabet, numerals; box-shaped buildings and exotic abstractions. Designs on the

The central section of the Manala village in the de Wildt district

Opposite Msiza the diviner taking leave of a patient

Entrance to a Manala homestead

Opposite A Manala matriarch inside her beautifully decorated home

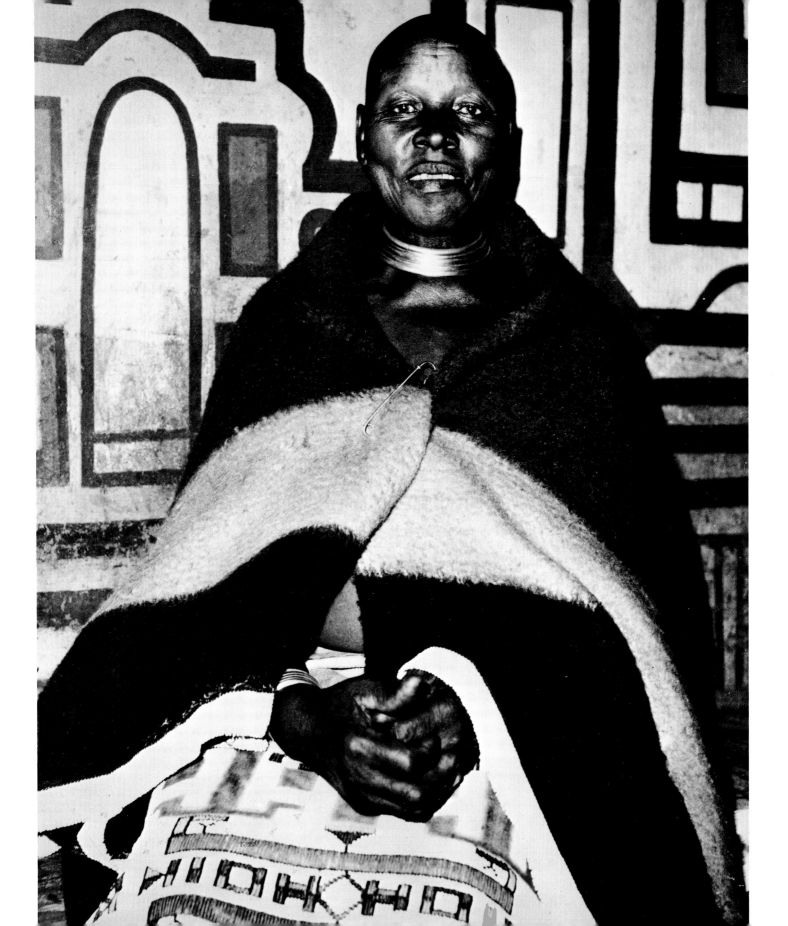

Most of the mural art is done during the dry winter months

The ornament maker

Body, neck and leg hoops

inner surfaces of courtyard walls, however, are plain, consisting mainly of straight, wavy or zigzag lines.

In distant times, the Manala relied exclusively on natural, indigenous pigments such as soot, ash and clay for the colours they used. Then with the arrival of traders in the Transvaal, they were introduced to household paints, and gradually their mural decorations began to change. Apart from the traditional colours the women could now use blues, greens, reds, browns, yellows and whites, thereby attaining new heights in creativity. Later, with the addition of courtyard archways, pilasters, cornices and other clay embellishments, their talents were to blossom as never before.

Manala villages became increasingly flamboyant, the most beautiful to be found in southern Africa.

Manala women devote their time to mural art in the autumn, when the day-to-day tasks in the maize and sorghum fields have come to an end, and to an even greater extent in winter when the rains have ceased and the crops have been harvested and stored. They also spend their leisure hours at beadwork, sitting together in the courtyards and relishing the mellow warmth of the winter's sun. Not that working with beads is confined to this time of the year. On the contrary, beadcraft is a cherished pastime even during spring and summer, when activities on the land are most demanding.

Beadcraft

The Ndebele woman's passion for personal adornment and her skill in beadcraft are rivalled in southern Africa only by her Zulu and Xhosa counterparts. However, nowhere south of the Zambezi river is there a larger range of ornaments worn by women than among the Manala, and indeed the Ndundza sections of this tiny and somewhat scattered tribal group.

Perhaps the most popular items of Ndebele ornamentation are the beaded hoops (*izixolwana*) worn by females after the age of puberty. These vary considerably in size, being fitted around the wrists, arms, ankles and legs, as well as the neck and stomach. They are made of thin stems of grass firmly sewn together to form a compact, circular core. This is then bound with strings of beads until the core has been completely covered. Narrow, tight-fitting ankle, wrist and neck hoops have to be made on the wearer's person, demanding extraordinary patience, while the broader ones that slip easily over feet, hands, head and shoulders are made apart and fitted afterwards.

Often several beaded hoops are worn on either leg, ranging in size from small to large according to the shape of the calf. They can be a hindrance to walking, not only because of their width but also their weight. Similar hoops are worn on the arms, often extending from wrist to shoulder with a gap left for the elbows.

The broad, tight-fitting neck-hoops, although extremely uncomfortable, are seen by Ndebele women as the most attractive and essential items of ornamentation. Worn year in and year out, these *izixolwana* press hard against the lower jaw, leading inevitably to a deformity of the mouth. This is because the pressure they exert is consistently transmitted to the upper jaw, causing the incisors and canines to splay and the lips to protrude.

For many years I had been baffled by this peculiarity among Manala and Ndundza women, and had tended to shrug it off as some obscure genetic phenomenon. It was only after coming into contact with a prominent orthodontist in Johannesburg, whose research among Africans had taken him to the Manala, that I realized the ornament most ardently admired by Ndebele women was the one they should in fact discard.

Virtually all Manala and Ndundza women wear heavy copper rings which can be opened and closed when heated and therefore fitted to size around the arms, legs and neck. While this is being done, the skin is protected with moistened rags, which are removed after the rings have cooled. Beaded hoops are worn over these rings, offsetting the relatively dull-surfaced metal with splashes of colour, albeit to the detriment of comfort.

Manala and Ndundza girls start wearing ornaments during early childhood – beaded anklets, wristlets, and necklaces. At this age, they are also dressed in a loin-flap (*legabe*), which consists of a little cascade of leather thongs attached to a waiststrap and tipped with beads. These hang loosely in front, covering the upper part of the thighs.

In adolescence, the *legabe* is replaced with a small apron (*phephethu*) which is covered from edge to edge with beads. In due course, this is replaced by the large, goat-skin apron (*maphotho*) worn exclusively by married women. Intricately decorated, mainly with white beads, the *maphotho* is broad, heavy and long and in some cases reaches down to the ankles. On the day of her marriage, a bride wears a veil of threaded beads, completely hiding her face. She is given an assortment of copper rings by the groom which she later has fitted to her legs, arms and neck by one of the female elders.

Traditionally the colours of beads had distinctive connotations, pointing largely to the stages of development in a person's life – infancy, childhood, puberty, betrothal, marriage and parenthood. They also reflected the mood of the maker – joy, sorrow, insecurity or impending good fortune. But as a result of contact with urban communities, connotations have undergone gradual change, and in certain cases have dwindled into obscurity. Interpretation of so-called 'messages' in beadwork can therefore be most misleading.

When I was probing the meanings of the colours in Ndebele beadwork in 1953, I was taken by Headman Msiza II to the oldest member of the village, a matriarch named Magogo. We found her in the courtyard of her home, shaving the head of a maiden, and therefore barely able to spare us a glance. A little later, when the job was done and she could talk to me, I was delighted to discover she was the great-great-granddaughter of Chief Nyabela, whose settlement I had explored in the Steenkamp mountains.

I learned from Magogo that white beads were regarded by both the Manala and Ndundza tribes as the most beautiful of all. White, she explained, stood for goodness, purity, love and protection, and was the dominant colour in all the finery worn on religious occasions. She was quick to explain that whereas some colours had pleasant connotations, others denoted unhappy and even evil situations. The greens and

Copper rings are difficult to fit and even more difficult to remove

Maiden of the Lobedu tribe in the North-Eastern
Transvaal. Like the Venda, the Lobedu were left
unscathed by the conqueror, Mzilikazi

A young woman of Headman Msiza's village near
de Wildt

Young married woman of the Manala tribe

The phenomenon of protruding teeth is common among Ndebele women. This is the result of continually wearing tight-fitting neck hoops

yellows were generally 'good' through their association with growth in spring, abundance in summer and the harvests in autumn. The blues were 'powerful' colours, because they were linked with the sea and sky, while the reds tended to suggest 'troubled times'. Opaque red beads, for example, which resemble blood, might be used to signify strife or heartache, while the transparent ones, being likened to fire or lightning, could hint at anger or a host of ominous events. Black, the darkest of all, represented sorcery, death and widowhood, while pink, as found in sea shells, was a sign of authority.

During times of mourning, the old lady continued, it was considered wrong for women to wear beads. All hoops had therefore to be removed and stored. Widows always stripped their marriage aprons of beads, and confined ornamental dress to copper rings.

After about an hour together in the courtyard, Magogo invited me into her hut, where she proudly showed me a range of ornaments and garments she herself had made and worn in the course of some forty years. Opening a kist in which they had been carefully stored, she brought out a blanket which I recognized as the one most commonly worn by Manala women on ceremonial and festive occasions. Magogo spread it out on the floor of the hut, carefully smoothing the folds in order best to display the woven bands of yellow, blue, red and mauve, as well as the miscellany of beads she had diligently sewn into the lower section. This part of the blanket consisted of row upon row of multi-coloured, geometric patterns boldly fringed with strips of white. As I look back now on that day, and then reflect on all the tribal finery I have seen in southern Africa, I rate this garment, this showpiece of Ndebele female dress, by far the most beautiful of all.

Among the other beaded items in Magogo's kist was a large assortment of hoops; a narrow, white head-band (*majegane*), a broad breast-belt and two long, snake-like cords (*izinyogo*) worn by mothers as a headdress when attending the wedding of a son. There was also a multi-beaded ox-horn snuff box and a dancing stick, as well as no less than a dozen different necklaces. Finally Magogo gave me an assegai blade to inspect, explaining it was an heirloom her grandmother had used specifically for shaving maidens' heads.

In the years following my first meeting with Magogo, I was to spend at least a half an hour with her whenever I visited Msiza II's magnificent village. Two months before her sudden death in 1963, she gave me an old *mophotho* apron, four of the hoops she had worn in her youth and a large assortment of beadwork. She is still remembered by the Manala with reverence, not only because she was the last of Chief Nyabela's elderly descendants, but also because she had shared her knowledge of beadcraft with virtually every woman of the village. No one could rival her extraordinary skill, the Manala say, no one could make beadwork look more beautiful.

Manala beadwork – a circle of women enjoying a leisurely conversation

The village dancers

Magogo, matriarch of
the Manala village,
and direct descendant
of Chief Nyabela

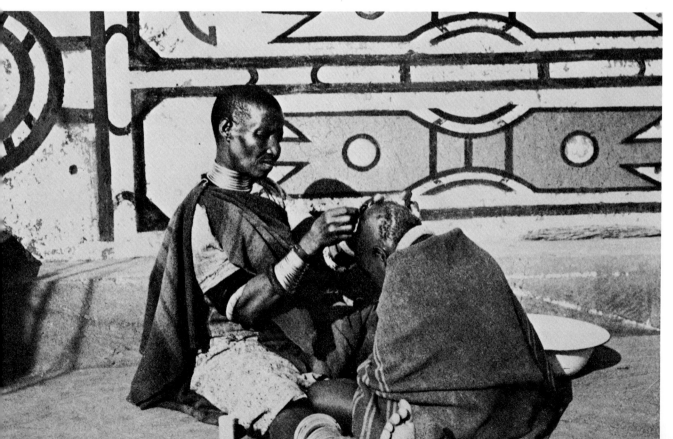

Magogo shaving the
head of a maiden

Manala women and children

In discussions I had with Headman Msiza over the years, he confessed he knew little about beads and other ornaments traditionally worn by men. This, he explained, was because Manala men had adopted European modes of dress, even before his birth. What little had survived was worn almost exclusively by a handful of medicine men. As Msiza himself was a medicine man, it seemed strange to me, after having known him for so many years, that I had never seen him dressed in distinctive regalia. One day, when I asked him why, he admitted he had a special outfit which he wore only on important ceremonial occasions, or when clients from far-off villages came to consult him.

'This I'll show you,' he promised, 'when the time is right.'

One morning in 1965, having just arrived in Msiza's village, I found him examining a goat that had been bitten to death by a dog from a neighbouring village.

'The owner is unwell,' Msiza said to me, 'so I've arranged for his wife to come and discuss the matter with me.

'I'd like you to be present and bring your cameras with you,' he added to my surprise. 'In the meantime, I suggest you visit other parts of the village; I'll send for you when I'm ready.'

I was summoned by Msiza during the afternoon, and barely recognized him when I reached his courtyard. He was fully dressed in the special regalia he had told me about. On his shaven head was a solitary ball of monkey fur, and around his neck hung strings of beads, a snuffbox and several duiker horns containing indigenous medicines. He wore a calfskin kilt, home-made sandals and ankle and waist bands clustered with moth cocoons. On his lap were two red roosters given him by the woman as compensation for the death of the goat.

Msiza and the woman conversed quietly, exchanging pinches of snuff as I prepared to photograph them. Half an hour later, the deliberations over, they repaired to the courtyard gates where they paused to greet each other. The roosters, although firmly held against Msiza's body, had shown few signs of discontent during the conversation.

Opposite

Manala children

Pepetwana Skosana,
custodian of Chief
Nyabela's old
settlement, wearing
his *dambo* necklace

However, when Msiza suddenly raised a hand in salute, they flicked their heads inquisitively from side to side, and then burst into a duet of cackling.

I took leave of Msiza towards evening, and was accompanied on my homeward journey by a pied kid goat which Msiza had sent as a gift for Peter, my son.

Unfortunately Msiza never saw the photographs I took of him in his special regalia. He died before my next visit to his village.

Skosana's Dambo

During my third visit to the ruins and caves of Chief Nyabela's settlement in the Steenkamp mountains in March 1976, I confessed to Skosana that I found it difficult to understand why Ndebele women should be so obsessed with personal adornment, while their menfolk appeared to have forsaken every vestige of traditional dress.

'It is true that we men no longer dress as our ancestors did,' he said with a smile, pensively stroking his beard, 'but not true to say that Ndebele men wear no ornaments at all.

'Most men have to wear charms from time to time,' he added, 'and these may be small and plain and newly made, or big and beautiful and very old.'

Skosana now unbuttoned and removed his shirt, revealing an exotic necklace which hung down to his navel.

'This is a charm I always wear,' he continued, 'but unlike the hoops and rings and other things you see on our women, it is not meant for everyone's eyes. It's my *dambo*, and can be worn only by me.'

'*Dambo*?' I queried.

'That's right,' he said, 'and although the word *dambo* means a dance, it is also the necklace that reminds one to keep in touch with one's ancestors.'

'The beads are uncommon,' I ventured.

'They are,' he replied, 'because they were given to me in an uncommon way – by my old father after his death.

'You see,' Skosana continued, 'when my father died his personal *dambo* became the property of my elder brother, which meant I didn't have one of my own. Then one night, shortly after we had come out of mourning, the old man appeared to me in a dream, saying: "Pepetwana, my son, go up the path to Chief Nyabela's old village, and if you search among the stones in the caves, you will find what you need for making your *dambo*." So that is exactly what I did.

'I searched and searched in the caves for many days and, finding nothing, began to fear I had imagined the dream. Then, after staying away from the caves for a week, I went again to search. This time I squeezed through a narrow tunnel into a part I had not been to before, and which I found to be dripping with water. There in the light of my torch I saw a pile of stones, and beside it some broken clay pots. Then scratching with my stick among the pieces, and digging in the soft, wet soil, I suddenly found the beads coming out, and then more and more as I continued to dig. I was so happy I began to laugh and then to cry, taking no notice of the bats that were flying around me. This was how my *dambo* beads were given to me...by my father after his death.'

In closely examining Skosana's necklace, I discovered it consisted of eighty-six beads (the ones he had found in the caves) as well as three chips of sweet-smelling *umthombothi* wood, eight rectangular strips of bone, nine blunted porcupine quills, five fragments of ostrich eggshell, and two pieces of tortoise shell. Finally, there was a cartridge case and a horn tip, both stuffed with indigenous medicines. He told me that the other items had been selected for him by a local medicine man. They provided the necklace with additional magical properties.

Like Pepetwana Skosana, I tend to believe in dreams, particularly the kind that engage the mind during waking hours. The habit of daydreaming invariably takes root in one's formative years, and in my own case was inspired by an Ndebele greybeard – the narrator, Sipho Mncube. It has taken me first in thought and then in person to far-off places, always in the belief that some dreams come true. For what other reason would I have explored the ruins of Chief Nyabela's settlement, or searched for old Sipho among the Ndundza people around Roossenekal, or visited and revisited the beautiful Manala village in the vicinity of de Wildt? How else would I have come to know Msiza II, Magogo, Skosana and many others who have made research among the Ndebele so very worthwhile?

The Northern Transvaal

THE MATABELE

Sipho Mncube always spoke of Mzilikazi, founder of the Matabele dynasty, as the greatest black southern African conqueror of the nineteenth century. In 1819, at the age of twenty-nine, Mzilikazi was one of King Shaka's regimental commanders, as well as his closest friend.

He was formerly chief of the Northern Khumalo, one of the smaller East Coast tribes, and had established himself as an indomitable Zulu warrior, a shrewd tactician and a leader whose extraordinary zeal could turn even faint-hearted men into formidable adversaries. And yet he was subject to spells of insecurity, his mind fraught with suspicions that sprang from the turbulent circumstances of the Shakan era. He is said, for instance, to have feared that some of the Zulu dignitaries would turn against him because of the prestige he had won and the privileges he enjoyed as the King's confidant. He very definitely feared that sooner or later he might fall into disfavour with the king himself, as had happened to several of Shaka's other associates. It is not surprising therefore that he planned to flee from KwaZulu as others had done. In any case, it grieved him to be serving a master, when he saw himself as the one to be served.

In June 1822, having been sent by Shaka at the head of two regiments to attack and subjugate a Sotho chief in the west, Mzilikazi surreptitiously collected his Khumalo subjects and took them with him. After defeating the Sotho chief and looting his village as planned, he continued westwards and crossed the Drakensberg mountains accompanied by his warriors and an estimated three hundred women and children.

Entering the Transvaal highveld, the Khumalo fell upon indefensible Sotho villages in the Ermelo district, and wrought havoc among the inhabitants. Farther to the north, where Sotho habitations were more plentiful, they carved a bloody path across the flats. As the local populace fled before them, the Khumalo pillaged their granaries, rounded up abandoned cattle and set about capturing young Sotho male and female fugitives. Mzilikazi urgently needed these captives. He would turn the men into army recruits, and present the maidens to his warriors as concubines.

By the end of 1823, Mzilikazi and his followers had reached the Steelpoort river, and during the following year they entered the hill-studded bushveld in the upper regions of the Olifants river. In those serene surroundings the young conqueror decided to remain a while. With the help of his warriors and the Sotho captives, he built a settlement of

The abaKwaZulu were
referred to by the inland
Sotho tribes as 'those
who sank out of sight'
behind their mighty
shields

beehive huts near the river. He named it ekuPumuleni – the Place of Rest.

But at ekuPumuleni there was to be no rest for Mzilikazi and his people. They were constantly harried by the Phuthing and other neighbouring tribes, and many of their cattle were stolen by the subjects of the most powerful of all African rulers in the north – Sekwati, supreme chief of the Pedi tribes. Incensed, Mzilikazi dispatched a fighting force to dislodge Sekwati from the mountain fortress on which he lived. This was to prove a humiliating experience for Mzilikazi and his warriors, their first since leaving KwaZulu.

Not only were they fiercely repulsed by Sekwati's army, they were also jeered at from the hilltops as they trudged back to the Place of Rest.

Since their arrival among the inland tribes, Mzilikazi's followers, recently renamed abaKwaZulu – The People of KwaZulu – had relied entirely on pillaging for food. But by 1824 their failure to subjugate both the Phuthing and Pedi tribes had led to a shortage of grain in the Place of Rest, and they were forced to look elsewhere for a source of supply. Mzilikazi decided to send a reconnoitring party to the west, where the terrain was said to be less rugged and Sotho

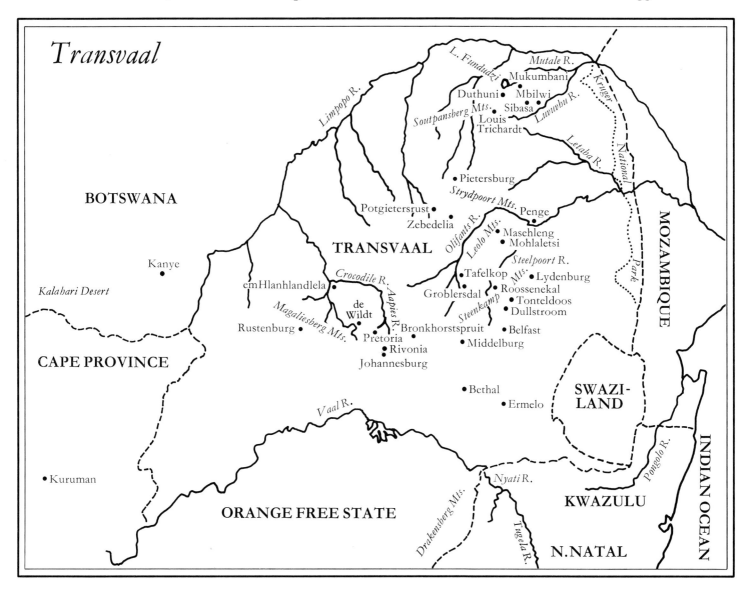

habitations plentiful. Soon the abaKwaZulu were detected by scouts of the prosperous Sotho-speaking Kwena (Crocodile People) in the vicinity of present-day Pretoria and Rustenburg. Their presence was regarded as ominous.

Returning to the Place of Rest, members of the reconnoitring party enthusiastically reported that they had found a territory where village granaries bulged with an over-abundance of grain, where the cultivated lands were lush with corn, and where the bushy pastures swarmed not only with cattle but also antelope. Mzilikazi was intrigued. In the autumn of 1825, he decided to abandon the Place of Rest, and move his abaKwaZulu into the territory of the Crocodile People.

On reaching the Magaliesberg mountains north of where Pretoria stands today, Mzilikazi quickly established a temporary settlement for his subjects, and then sent his regiments on a series of marauding expeditions against the Crocodile People. This tribe, he was soon to discover, like other Sotho-speaking tribes he had encountered in the Ermelo district, was unaccustomed to organized warfare and was ignorant of the art of hand-to-hand combat.

The abaKwaZulu overran the Kwena villages. Then they collected the spoils of war as they had done two years before – great quantities of grain, large herds of cattle and the cream of Kwena youth. By the end of the year, Mzilikazi had reduced the once prosperous Crocodile People to a state of poverty. He had also proclaimed himself supreme ruler over all their territories, and the abaKwaZulu as their overlords.

During most of 1826 the abaKwaZulu devoted their attention to building family settlements in their new domain. In addition, three military settlements were founded along the banks of the Aapies river, and several cattleposts established in the bushveld regions between the Magaliesberg range and Limpopo river. Meanwhile the Crocodile People had started referring to the abaKwaZulu as 'Matabele', meaning roughly 'They who sink out of sight (-tebele)' behind their shields. They spoke of the Matabele as an invincible people, and Mzilikazi as a despot with an insatiable lust for power.

At the beginning of 1827, the Matabele army consisted of no less than eight regiments, five of which Mzilikazi had earmarked for service against neighbouring tribes yet to be conquered. In April, he sent an expeditionary force to the north on a mission of destruction. By the end of August it had not only succeeded in destroying villages as far afield as the Limpopo river, but had also returned to Pedi territory and defeated Sekwati's army in a bloody struggle. Three years before the abaKwaZulu had been humiliated by the Pedi 'rock rabbits', as Mzilikazi had called them. They were now his vassals. Their power had been decisively broken.

Mzilikazi's awesome reputation as a conqueror spread rapidly across central South Africa. Within the next decade he established himself as ruler over all the indigenous peoples outside the Lesotho, KwaZulu and the Cape Province. All, that is, except the small Venda tribe that inhabited a remote mountainous region in the North-Eastern Transvaal, and its neighbours, the Lobedu, whose queen, Modjadji I, he judiciously avoided antagonizing.

Although my interest in Mzilikazi had been kindled by Sipho Mncube during my childhood years, it was only in 1958, following a commission by a British publisher to write the conqueror's biography, that I began making a detailed study of his many-faceted career. This demanded exhaustive scrutiny of archival material – diaries, letters and other documents left to posterity by missionaries, traders, hunters and adventurers who had known Mzilikazi and befriended him. It also meant following the trail the conqueror had carved through southern Africa, starting from his birthplace in KwaZulu and ending at emHlanhlandela beyond the Limpopo river, where he died in 1868.

During my travels I came into contact with the various tribes Mzilikazi had conquered, first in central South Africa, then in Botswana and finally in regions as far to the north as the Zambezi river. In discussions with innumerable tribal chroniclers, I was able to record not only their descriptions of Mzilikazi's escapades, but also their assessment of his character and stature as an African conqueror. From this research came the book, *Path of Blood – The Rise and Conquests of Mzilikazi, Founder of the Matabele.*

THE PEDI

While the Ndebele remained unmolested by the Matabele, the lot of the Pedi was different. The Matabele yoke of subjugation weighed so heavily upon them, that they added a lament to some of their age-old songs: *Mosegare maahlo a rena a tletse dikeledi, re robala ka tlala* (By day our eyes are in tears, by night we sleep in hunger.)

Mzilikazi, the conqueror, located the Sotho-
speaking tribes in the most rugged parts of the
Northern Transvaal

They were, however, freed of Mzilikazi's oppression in
1836, after the defeat and dispersal of the Matabele by the
Boers, and emerged again as an independent tribal group,
gradually retrieving their erstwhile prosperity. When I
visited their villages between the upper Olifants and
Steelpoort rivers in 1958, I found it difficult to visualize the
tribulation that had once pervaded the territory. Few of the
Pedi chroniclers were prepared to admit Mzilikazi had been
their overlord. They spoke of him as a hyena that had
ventured into Pedi territory, only to be mauled by the
mightiest of lions, their illustrious father, Chief Sekwati.

Pedi territory is known to its inhabitants as Bopedi – Place of
the Pedi – and yet of the 120 tribes who people it, only nine
are truly Pedi. The Sotho-speaking Koni, Roka, Tau and
Kwena groups account for eighty-five tribes. The remainder
stem from various origins.

In July 1958 my research into Mzilikazi's life and conquests began in earnest. After two weeks in KwaZulu and
another in the Ermelo district, I reached Bopedi, where I
headed for Mohlaletsi, royal village of Chief Moroamache
Sekhukhune. Sprawled across bushy, rolling terrain in the
western foothills of the Leolo mountains, the settlement

Village in the upper regions of the Olifants river

Outskirts of a village in the foothills of the Leolo
mountains

consisted of hundreds of homesteads, and was scarred with goat and cattle trails, footpaths and wagon roads and deeply eroded gullies. In summer Mohlaletsi can be hot, humid and extremely muddy after the rains. But as I arrived in midwinter, at the height of the dry season, I found it cold and bleak and shrouded in wind-swept dust.

I had written to Chief Sekhukhune a month before, asking his permission to research in the village and interview chroniclers, and so I drove straight to his home. But the chief was away. He had gone to Masehleng, another royal village farther to the north, and was not expected back until the following day. He had, however, arranged for an elder of the tribe, Kgobalala Sekhukhune, to act as my host and mentor. I was taken by a councillor to the old man's home, where I was shown to a bench beneath a thorntree and told to wait. I was shivering now, for there was a bite in the wind, and the sun had been reduced to a hazy orb behind the clouds of dust.

Ten minutes later Kgobalala appeared. Leaning heavily on a stick, he wore a heavy khaki overcoat, the collar upturned to cover his cheeks, a broad-brimmed hat, woollen gloves and dark, metal-framed spectacles. At first glance, there was little I could see of his face, except his nose, his grey moustache and smiling teeth.

'*Tobela morena*,' he cried, greeting me in typical Pedi fashion. 'The air is cold but our hearts are warm, so you'll be warmly received by the people of Mohlaletsi.

'You have been here before?' the old man asked.

'No,' I replied.

'Then I'm glad you've come with a desire to learn,' he said, 'especially as there is so much to be learnt in Mohlaletsi.'

Kgobalala assured me he had arranged for a group of elderly men to meet me for discussion on Mzilikazi's role in Pedi history.

'However,' he continued, 'before we start talking about olden times, it is important you see how we live today. I'll introduce you first to my friend, Motubatze, who will be pleased to show you around.'

A few minutes later Kgobalala and I set out in my truck for Motubatze's place. Following a narrow track through the village we soon reached a ridge which was topped with precipices, studded with boulders and tufted with thornbush and flowering aloes. Following its base was a seemingly unending line of Pedi homesteads. One of them, fronted with syringa trees and line upon line of aloes in bloom, belonged to Motubatze.

'This is my friend's *kgoro*,' Kgobalala said as we drew up beneath the syringa trees. 'And by *kgoro* we mean not only the place where a man, his family and others live, but also the big enclosure where the cattle are kept and gatherings are held.'

We were met by Motubatze at the entrance of the *kgoro*. He was about sixty years old. Plump and jovial, he seemed the kind of man who could face most challenges of life without undue concern. Inviting us into the *kgoro*, Motubatze led us to a thorntree where a small circle of men sat warming themselves beside a fire. I discovered later that these were the chroniclers Kgobalala had spoken about, and I spent the following day with them at the fireside.

When I look back now on my first visit to Pedi country and others that followed in the 1960s, I regard Motubatze's *kgoro* as a good example of an average Pedi homestead. It consisted of two main sections – a circular enclosure made of thorntree branches, and behind it the living quarters comprising seventeen rondavel homes built side by side in semicircular formation. This section was subdivided into five family units, each isolated from the others by tall, encompassing walls.

Within the enclosed section of the *kgoro* the village cattlefolds are situated. This is where selected animals are sheltered at nights, and where the cows are milked in the mornings and evenings. The cattlefold is also the place where *kgoro* patriarchs are buried, where religious ceremonies are performed and where animals are slaughtered at times of festivity. As among other southern African tribes, the Pedi cattlefold is restricted to males. Women are forbidden to come into contact with cattle, or even to handle the milkers' thongs, milking stools or pails.

The fireplace within the enclosed section of the *kgoro* is also taboo for women. Situated to the right of the main entrance, it is usually partly sheltered by a low stone wall. Here the menfolk gather to discuss domestic or tribal matters, to settle disputes, to yarn over a pot of home-brewed beer or to recount the heroic deeds of Pedi warriors of bygone days. It is also the place where the first portions of the harvest are ceremoniously cooked, where dances are held and where male visitors to the *kgoro* are made to feel welcome.

My fireside discussion with the chroniclers began, as arranged, on the morning after my arrival at the Mohlaletsi *kgoro*. All elderly dignitaries, they were gifted speakers who derived great pleasure in expounding personal theories about Mzilikazi's conquests. They were quick to agree, or to disagree, with some of the opinions I ventured to offer on what had transpired in Bopedi after the founding of the

The cattlefold serves many purposes, but may only be entered by males

conqueror's settlement, the Place of Rest. They were unanimous in their condemnation of Mzilikazi's ruthlessness, albeit in fairness they did concede to his greatness in emerging from obscurity to found the most powerful of all southern African inland tribes – the Matabele.

In meeting the chroniclers, I was able to add a number of valuable facts to the material I had already gleaned from archival sources. More important, they helped dispel some of the fanciful notions I had developed about Mzilikazi from stories told to me by Sipho Mncube.

A Kwena homestead,
Moletji village

Cowdung is extensively used as fuel. It is also
used for plastering floors and walls

THE KWENA OF MOLETJI

One of my favourite haunts in the Northern Transvaal is the Moletji district, in the region of Pietersburg, a vast sun-baked territory interwoven with mountain ranges, weather-battered cliffs, scraggy bush and grasslands roamed by cattle, donkeys, goats and sheep. The Moletji village, capital of one of the Kwena tribes, lies huddled in a sultry hollow fringed with granite hills. It is the headquarters of a young, soft-spoken chief named Kgabo Moloto whose lineage boasts an imposing succession of ancestral rulers.

Like the Pedi, the Kwena live in thatched rondavel homes which face into a courtyard lined with walls. Cattlefolds and goatpens built either of stones or thorntree branches are situated near the courtyard gates. Close by are the maize, sorghum and pumpkin gardens which the Kwena fence with poles cut from the *magorogoro* tree. These poles are preferred to others because they begin to grow soon after planting, developing a strong root-structure, and sprouting branches to form a hedge.

The Kwena, often mistakenly referred to as one of the Pedi tribes, are in fact of Tswana stock; they migrated in distant times from the west to the vicinity of Pietersburg. Most Moletji families claim to be linked by kinship ties, some closely and others remotely, by virtue of their common ancestry. This bond, however tenuous, is symbolized in Moletji territory by a crocodile totem, which is conspicuously displayed especially on ceremonial occasions. This practice is not exclusive to the Kwena. The Pedi, for example, recognize the porcupine as their totem, the Tau the lion; the Phiri the hyena; the Tlaru the python and the Tlokwa the wild cat, to name but a few.

Groups of people who recognize a common totem usually have set standards to uphold. They are expected to stand together in times of misfortune, always to be hospitable and kind to each other, and when journeying in a group to far-off places, to share their provisions. Until relatively recent times, the killing and eating of totem animals was strictly taboo. Even touching a totem could provoke the ancestral spirits to retribution. Despite these spiritual overtones, totemism has no deep-rooted religious significance. It merely indicates the high degree of gregariousness in the social structure of Sotho-speaking peoples.

Moletji Shrines

In all tribal habitations, there are special places dedicated by families to their ancestors. In some areas these are situated within a hut, and in others in the cattlefold or beside a village gate. The most sacred spot in a Moletji household is a circular, concave shrine. Made of clay and plastered with cowdung, it forms part of the courtyard floor. It is the place where members of a family make regular contact with their guardian ancestors, and where they are sometimes joined in worship by neighbouring kinsmen and friends.

At the beginning of 1975 I accepted an offer by a film company in Johannesburg to write and host a series of television programmes to be entitled *The Tribal Identity*. I set out with Lionel Friedberg the film director and his camera crew for Venda in July. There we filmed various aspects of Venda culture, including initiation ceremonies for boys and girls. By October we had completed our work among the Venda, and had moved into the Pietersburg district, arriving in due course at the Moletji village. As methods of worship formed part of the series, I had decided to visit some of the shrines in the neighbourhood. Kgabo Moloto, chief of the Kwena, appointed three guides to help us, the oldest and most senior of whom was a grey-haired councillor named Frans Phoko.

Our introduction to a Moletji shrine took place in Frans Phoko's courtyard. Growing from its centre were two bulbs in bloom, which Phoko described as his ancestors. While Friedberg and his assistants set up the cameras and other equipment, I asked the old man to explain the significance of the bulbs to me.

'As I have said, these are my ancestors,' Phoko began, 'which I'm sure you find difficult to understand.

'Now this bulb with red flowers,' he continued, 'is known as *legwama*, and grows in all parts of Kwena country. However, when it is grown in a shrine, we call it *Mokgalabye*, which means 'old man', because within it there is life, and that life is the spirit of my ancestral grandfather. Other families in the village have similar shrines and *legwama* bulbs, all representing an old man in the world of ancestors to whom they can pray and ask for help.

'When we pray at this shrine, my family and I, we talk to this plant, addressing it as Kwena Phoko because these were

Phoko of Moletji village

my grandfather's names. And we thank him for heeding our prayers, or ask him to cure our illnesses, or to send us rain, or to keep our cattle free from disease. We ask him for many things.

'This other plant with the yellow flower,' said Phoko, pointing to the second bulb, 'also grows everywhere in Moletji. Out in the veld and the bush we know it as *tuntwane*, but here in the shrine it is *Mosadi Mogolo* – the old lady. This is because within it is the spirit of my ancestral grandmother, and among other families the spirit of theirs.

'So we look carefully after the two plants of our shrines,' Phoko concluded, 'knowing that even in the winter, when their leaves have died and their flowers have gone they are still alive. Just as alive as we know our ancestors to be.'

Phoko's shrine, I was later to discover when we called on some of his friends, was basically the same as others in the village. Without exception they were neatly kept, and the bulbs were on the brink of flowering. In one of the courtyards, the shrine was covered with a variety of items – a ring of plaited sticks called *moraro*, shreds of red bark (*mahawane*), shavings of *mahegeta* bark and sprinklings of snuff.

At another home we arrived in the courtyard just as the owner, a very old patriarch, was pouring a calabash of water over his shrine. Standing beside him was a little bare-footed boy, his eyes half closed and his lips whispering an inaudible prayer. Suddenly the two of them sank to their knees, leaned forward and drank of the water that had gathered around the bulbs.

'They are both unwell,' Phoko whispered to me, 'but soon they'll be healed...thoroughly healed by the old man's ancestral grandparents whose fingers have touched the water they drink.'

Phoko's shrine

All tribal groups in southern Africa acknowledge a Supreme Being whose workings are so great and whose abode is so remote as to defy the comprehension of man. This Supreme Being is known by different names in the various vernacular languages – *Nkulunkulu* (Zulu), *Qamatha* (Xhosa), *Kalunga* (Vambo), *Raluvhimba* (Venda) and *Molimo* (Sotho) – and is generally accepted as the creator of the universe, the provider of foodstuffs, indigenous medicines and natural resources and the controller of lightning, thunder, rain, hail, floods and drought.

But although the concept of the Supreme Being forms the basis of traditional tribal religion, no rituals or ceremonies are directed to its worship. Traditional religious practices are governed by a belief in the survival of the soul after death, its departure to a realm of ancestors and its subsequent influence on the destinies of kinsmen left behind.

Respondents are inclined to be vague when describing the whereabouts of the realm of ancestors. Among the various tribes it is believed to be remotely situated in an ethereal domain, or underground, or in sacred forests, groves and mountain ranges, or in the vicinity of specified lakes, rivers and waterfalls. There seems to be no doubt, however, as to the nature of life after death. Although perceived as fundamentally similar to earthly life, it is considerably less arduous and certainly more prosperous.

One of the more elaborate Moletji shrines. The central *legwama* bulb is embraced by plaited sticks and other magical items

Malatji the Medicine Man

On the morning of our third day in the Moletji village, Phoko suggested we visit the home of Lucas Malatji, one of the best-known medicine men in the territory.

'This *ngaka* [medicine man],' said Phoko, 'has been greatly blessed by his ancestors for many years. He's a happy man with happy ways and a gift for making his patients feel just as happy. He cures their ailments, always smiling, interprets their dreams, always with accuracy, and in advising them how to avoid or overcome the misfortunes of life, he always speaks words of wisdom. He is the kind of man one likes to visit for the sake of visiting, and even more so in times of trouble.'

Phoko was right. We had hardly drawn up at Malatji's place – it consisted of a small rectangular home flanked on either side by rondavel huts – than he came striding across the courtyard, smiling broadly, to welcome us. Reaching the gate, and recognizing Phoko, he hailed us with outstretched arms. He was stockily built, about forty-five years old and had a voice that was deep and arresting. He wore a khaki shirt, khaki trousers, brown shoes, a headdress made of oxtail hair and a leopard skin that covered his shoulders and back, the tail-tip almost reaching the ground.

Malatji led us to the rectangular house and, ushering us into a dusky room, invited us to sit down with him at a table laden with herbs, roots, leaves and other medicinal paraphernalia. During the following five minutes, he and Phoko talked alone, enquiring after the health of their respective families, and diligently exchanging items of news about mutual friends. Then, told by Phoko of our activities during the past three days, Malatji straightened in his chair and, with a nod of the head, declared he was pleased we had come to see him. He said he would gladly answer whatever questions I might wish to ask him. Later he would go into the courtyard where Friedberg could film him treating a patient.

opposite The beaded blankets worn by Manala women are among the most beautiful in Southern Africa

Malatji the medicine man of Moletji village

'You are a healer?' I began, switching on my tape recorder.

'Yes,' he replied, 'but I must tell you from the start that it is not so much I, myself, who does the healing, but my ancestors who always work with me. This is important, and must be understood.

'You see,' said Malatji, 'very many patients come to me each day, but before speaking to them about their ailments, I get them to sit with me while I throw *ditaola* [divinatory bones] and consult my ancestors for guidance. In this way I quickly discover what kind of problem a patient has, the cause behind it, what treatment is needed, and whether in fact I can help at all. This is because some patients are meant to be healed straight away, some after a week or two and others not at all, meaning that their time for dying has come. Success or failure depends largely on what the ancestors decide, so a healer like myself knows how to be thankful when his patients are cured.

'Now when you consider the many kinds of ailments that people have – headaches, stomach and liver complaints, aching joints, fear of bewitchment, and so on, it stands to reason that medicine men soon learn from experience that they are more successful with some of their treatments than they are with others. So they begin to specialize, giving treatment only to patients whom they know in advance they are likely to cure. I myself have an understanding of many illnesses, so I don't have to specialize in just one or two. For this I am deeply thankful, never forgetting that I'm merely a tool in the hands of my healing ancestors.'

A young woman wearing a yellow turban and a floral dress now entered the room. Making obeisance to Malatji, and speaking in little more than a whisper, she reported that a patient had arrived and wanted to see him urgently. So, excusing himself, Malatji left us and went into the courtyard.

While waiting with Phoko in the dusky room, I recalled Malatji's comments about the influence of the ancestors on his role as a *ngaka*. Malatji was a versatile practitioner, I told myself, for not only did he make use of divinatory bones as a diagnostic aid, he was also said to be an outstanding herbalist. It was not usual for a *ngaka* to be adept in both divination and the use of indigenous medicines. Normally a diviner's task was confined to interpreting the reasons for a patient's illness or other misfortunes, and then, more specifically, the extent to which this stemmed from the anger of the ancestors, or the insidious activities of a witch or sorcerer. Here his function usually ended. Thereafter, a patient would need a herbalist to give him curative, indigenous medicines, should he be physically unwell, or protective charms or magical potions if he was psychologically disturbed. Lucas Malatji, who bestrode both these spheres of traditional medical practice, was therefore exceptionally gifted.

My thoughts were interrupted by the beating of drums and, rising quickly, I accompanied Phoko and the others into the courtyard. We found Malatji, battle-axe in hand, seated on a chair among three female drummers who burst into song at a sign from the *ngaka*. Directly opposite Malatji, a young man sat cross-legged on the courtyard floor. Head bowed and fingers nervously twitching, his impassive eyes were fixed on a small reed mat which Malatji had placed before him. With a nod from the *ngaka* both the drumming and singing ceased. Now Malatji told the patient to open his hands and filled them with an assortment of divinatory bones which he shook from a little skin bag.

'Breathe over them,' cried Malatji, 'and then throw them on to the mat. Whatever your troubles may be, my friend, these *ditaola* will guide us in what to do.'

As soon as the young man had cast the bones, Malatji, leaning forward, carefully studied the positions into which they had rolled. Then, clearing his throat, he sat back in his chair and addressed the patient.

'You are ill,' he said.

The young man nodded.

'You have an aching head and your eyes are sore. Do you agree?'

'I agree,' replied the young man, nodding again.

'This began last night; am I right?'

'You are right.'

'You woke up from a dream, feeling ill?'

'I did.'

'And in your dream you saw an ancestor?'

'Yes.'

'Your father?'

'Yes.'

'And in seeing him you knew he had something to tell you?'

'Yes.'

'But before he could speak you were already awake?'

'Yes, I woke up feeling cold with sweat.'

'Cold with sweat but also with an aching head and very sore eyes?'

'Both very sore, my head and my eyes.'

A patient consulting *Ngaka* Malatji

The dance begins

The dance over, the patient moves to the opposite side of the mat

'So now you are puzzled about dreaming of your father, and then waking to find yourself feeling ill?'

'Very puzzled, because never before has this happened to me, and I keep on wondering if I have offended my father, and if perhaps he has plans to punish me.'

'No, no my son,' interjected Malatji, 'you have nothing to fear. Because from what I see in the bones, your father is not angry but pleased with you, and had sought merely to let you know you were going to be ill. Do you not see, young man, that even as you slept he knew you were ill, and had you continued to dream, he would have told you so? He would also have suggested you visit a *ngaka* like myself, and get medicines to make you feel well again.

'Do you believe that by coming to me you were sent by him?' Malatji asked.

'I truly believe,' the patient replied.

'Then you must also believe you have nothing to fear, and much to be thankful for. Because presently I'll be giving you medicines that will quickly rid your body of bile, making you feel well and strong again as you're accustomed to be. In fact, tonight you'll fall quickly asleep, dreaming happily and undisturbed.'

A look of relief crept over the young man's face and, pressing his hands together in front of his chest, he said he was grateful for Malatji's help. Malatji then sprang to his feet and, holding the battle-axe aloft went loping around the courtyard. He eventually broke into a vigorous dance as the women began to sing again and to beat the drums. Moving his feet rapidly in a succession of little steps, his arms held high and his body swaying, he went skittering back and forth in front of the drummers. Next moment, he was twirling, crouching, leaping and stamping his feet, until finally he nimbly picked up the rhythm of the drums and danced back to his chair.

In the meantime, the young man had seated himself on the opposite side of the mat, where he pensively eyed the divinatory bones. He had taken little notice of Malatji's dancing, and hardly moved when it was over and the *ngaka* sat down behind him. This was his way of showing humility, Phoko later explained to me. After all, he was still feeling ill, and was probably not completely sure that Malatji's medicines would cure him.

When the drumming and the singing came to an end, Malatji led his patient into a nearby rondavel hut where he kept a vast assortment of bulbs, tubers, roots, bark, leaves, berries and other medicinal raw materials. They came out about ten minutes later and paused to discuss Malatji's fee for having thrown the bones and given the young man a handful of emetics, analgesics and laxatives.

'There will be no charge today,' Malatji said.

'No charge, my father?' the patient queried.

'No charge,' Malatji repeated.

The young man bowed low before the *ngaka*, deeply moved. Then, raising a hand in salute, he turned and padded out of the courtyard.

Sedimo

We took leave of Lucas Malatji after sharing a meal of boiled chicken and *moroho* (wild spinach) with him in his rectangular house. A chilly breeze had sprung up and a heavy mist sneaked through the village. In the early afternoon, we called on another of Phoko's friends who was also a healer and enjoyed an outstanding reputation as a medicine man. He was, however, not a diviner, but a specialist in *sedimo*.

In *sedimo* the patient's illness is diagnosed and then the symptoms are transferred into a goat or sheep. I had seen it performed in a Pedi settlement near Penge on the Olifants river in 1960, so now, fifteen years later, I was all the more delighted at the prospect of a similar experience. But to my great disappointment, I did not meet the *sedimo* medicine man of Moletji village personally. He was far too busy when we arrived at his home.

We found him in a rondavel hut, one of four facing inwards on to an empty courtyard. Seated on a stool within a circle of male spectators, he was carefully examining the swollen, arthritic hands, knees and ankles of a middle-aged man. Beside him stood a goat, its head erect and eyes inquisitively probing the shadowy darkness of the hut.

When the examination was over, the medicine man, leaning forward, placed a hand on the patient's shoulder.

'You have been suffering,' he said.

'Very greatly,' the patient replied.

'So you walk with a stick like a very old man, even though you are not yet old.'

The patient agreed.

'Do you believe in *sedimo*?'

'I do.'

'Do you really believe that your sickness can be transferred into this goat beside me, leaving you feeling better?'

'I do.'

'And what makes you so sure?'

Ndebele beadwork

The patient hesitated now, gathering his thoughts.

'I think it's because I have seen others cured in this way,' he explained. 'But in any case, I really believe I am meant to be cured.'

'You are,' said the medicine man, standing up. 'It is just that we cannot be certain when this will be – today, tomorrow or perhaps next year.'

He reached for a large skin bag from which he removed a smaller one containing indigenous medicines. Turning to the goat, he stroked its body with the second bag, softly calling upon the animal to fall asleep. Soon the goat, bleating forlornly, began to stagger. At once the medicine man toppled it over and made it lie outstretched on the floor facing the arthritic patient.

The patient was told to lie down beside the goat, and breathe heavily into its nostrils. There was no hurry, the medicine man said, as he covered both goat and patient with a woollen blanket. He insisted that the man should continue to 'breathe his sickness away' as he had directed, until the pain and stiffness had disappeared from his limbs. Should he feel no relief after about half an hour, he could then get up knowing that the time to be cured had not yet come.

During the next twenty-five minutes an atmosphere of solemn expectancy pervaded the hut. We watched in silence, not daring to speak lest we disturb the goat, distract the patient's attention or annoy the medicine man. I sensed we were instinctively united in willing the treatment to succeed. While we waited, my thoughts went back to 1960, and my introduction to *sedimo* near the Olifants river. The situation had been similar, except that then the goat had been unruly and more difficult to control. Besides, the patient, although in urgent need of help – he was old and dropsical – had been uncooperative, repeatedly objecting to sharing a blanket with an animal, any animal, let alone one as lowly as a goat. The interior of the hut had been as dark then as now, which made photography impossible. The use of flashlight was out of the question.

At a tap on my shoulder from Phoko I suddenly realized the patient had uncovered his head and chest, and was no longer breathing into the goat's nostrils. I watched carefully as he drew the blanket aside, sat up and began clenching and opening his hands. He then repeatedly bent and straightened his legs, flicked his feet from side to side and finally examined his knees and ankles, prodding them with his fingertips. Without the slightest sign of disappointment or pleasure, he rose to his feet, stepped once around the goat and, accompanied by the medicine man, walked out of the hut. We could hear them laughing together in the courtyard, which meant, according to Phoko, the patient was healed. I was delighted, especially as, fifteen years before at Penge, I had seen the treatment fail.

And what of the goat? It remained motionless beneath the blanket, silently sleeping, even though the hut had suddenly filled with voices as the spectators loudly discussed what had happened. After about an hour the medicine man returned. The patient, he told us, was resting outside. He had definitely benefited from the treatment, he said, and although his joints were still as swollen and stiff as before, the pain had now disappeared. He had been walking up and down the courtyard without his stick, as proof he no longer needed it.

A spectator asked why the goat had not yet woken up and the medicine man replied that, having been put to sleep, it could not wake up on its own. Only he himself had the power to do this.

'You try,' he said to one of the men, pulling the blanket aside and exposing the goat. 'Do what you like. Call it, kick it, dig it with a stick or prick it with a knife, just be sure not to injure it.'

The man stepped forward and, taking the goat by the hind legs, shook them violently. But the goat continued to sleep. A second man tapped its horns with a snuffbox, tugged its ears and opened its eyelids. It continued to sleep. Finally, a third man whacked it with his hand across the thigh. Nothing happened. Then the medicine man, chuckling triumphantly, stroked its body with the medicine bag he had used at the start of the treatment. About a minute later, the goat opened its eyes, lifted its head and struggled to its feet. Suddenly startled, it swung around, made a dash for the open door and landed with a leap in the courtyard. It was caught soon afterwards and slaughtered. The carcass was then skinned, cut into numerous portions and spread over the flames of a newly lit fire. First to eat of the roasted meat were the patient and the medicine man. What remained was then distributed among the rest of us.

It was past five o'clock when we withdrew from the feast and set out for Phoko's home. By now Moletji village was enveloped in mist and the air was moist and frosty. Earlier in the day we had passed innumerable villagers and animals along the track, so now our truck crept cautiously through the opaque surroundings.

A Sacrificial Ceremony

We had barely covered three kilometres when we came upon an old man and his wife and invited them to ride with us. They were on their way to a sacrificial ceremony at a home not far from Phoko's.

In tribal southern Africa, religious ceremonies are practised regularly throughout the year. They are widespread at the beginning of the planting season, in midsummer when the crops have ripened and again in autumn when harvests have been stored. In some parts it is customary for hoes to be ritually cleansed before the lands are tilled, and for special visits to be made to ancestral burial grounds before the sowing begins. It is common practice for incantations to be sung while melon seeds or grain from the previous year are sprinkled or ritually planted on selected graves. This is usually followed by prayers delivered to the shades of the dead. The ancestors are fervently asked to watch over the growing crops, to send bountiful rains, and to provide the villages with abundant harvests.

The most important agricultural ceremony held in the summer, the first fruits ceremony, may involve no more than a small circle of kinsmen and friends. On the other hand, it may demand the participation of many thousands of tribesmen, including chiefs, headmen, councillors, diviners and even dignitaries from neighbouring territories. But whether small or elaborate, the underlying principle of all first fruits ceremonies is fundamentally the same: none of the ripening crops may be eaten until offerings have been made and prayers of thanksgiving delivered to the appropriate ancestors.

In the same way harvest ceremonies held at the beginning of winter may be conducted domestically or on a national scale. They are accompanied by prayers and also singing, dancing, feasting and unbounded rejoicing.

The atmosphere at religious ceremonies is usually charged with conviviality, and prayers are delivered informally. The reason for this is the belief that, in moving into a new life after death, the ancestors retain most of their human characteristics. So they are praised and thanked during times of good fortune, but also criticized or reprimanded if they are thought to be neglecting their earthly descendants. Indeed, they are not infrequently cursed.

We entered an avenue of *marulla* trees and our attention was suddenly arrested by the beating of drums. This was the venue of the religious ceremony. With the old man to guide us, we left the truck, cut through the trees and drew up beside a courtyard gate. At that moment, the drumming stopped, mysteriously I thought, but we could hear a hubbub of voices. Friedberg, the camera crew and I waited at the gate while Phoko, the old man and his wife joined the throng in the courtyard. We were summoned not five minutes later, and introduced to the patriarch in charge of proceedings and the officiating diviner, Paulina Lephalala.

The courtyard was smaller than most I had seen in Moletji village. It was overcrowded with worshippers, although there were no more than sixty. We found the elderly owner of the homestead seated on a homemade chair outside the door of his hut. On his left was a group of turbanned women, most of them draped in colourful blankets; on his right a party of men, and, beside them, completing the circle of worshippers, some fifteen children of various ages. The whole gathering was happily engaged in conversation.

In southern Africa spring arrives in September, while October heralds the rainy season and the time for tilling and planting. At the time of our visit to Moletji in October 1975, the rains had not yet come; which accounts for the ceremony we were about to witness. It had been convened by the patriarch to make sacrifice to the ancestors, not only for his own benefit, but also on behalf of his relatives. Before our arrival at his home, a goat had been slaughtered, skinned, dismembered and offered in prayer to *Mokhalabye*, the ancestral grandfather whose lineage the worshippers shared. The old grandfather had been a kindly and generous man, the patriarch told me later, and although his death had caused untold sorrow, the mourners had found comfort in the thought that henceforth, as an ancestor, he could play an even more meaningful role in their lives.

'We have just been praying very hard to *Mokhalabye*,' the patriarch had said, 'pleading for him to remember us. Over and over pleading with him, making offerings of the slaughtered goat and then loudly singing:

Oh *Mokhalabye* we are offering you food today,
So please give us plenty back.
Plenty to eat in the summer
And to store for the winter.
So please don't forget us,
Always remembering to send us rain!'

The presiding patriarch takes a customary pinch of snuff before tasting the sorghum beer brewed for the ceremony

Worshippers take turns in making offerings of sorghum beer to the ancestors

opposite
A youthful worshipper sips sorghum beer from the courtyard floor

The skin of a sacrificial goat, a pot of sorghum beer mounted on a heap of sorghum dregs and the family shrine

I noticed that the skin of the sacrificial goat had been spread, fur downwards, on the floor of the courtyard and within the circle of worshippers. Beside it was a huge pot of frothy sorghum beer, its base placed firmly on a heap of dregs, sifted from the brew on the previous evening. Both the skin and the pot were close to a shrine in which the 'grandfather' and 'grandmother' bulbs had recently come into bloom.

While the worshippers continued to chat with each other, they took turns in making personal offerings to the ancestral grandfather. Coming forward one by one, they knelt beside the pot, scooped out a calabash of beer, carefully poured a little on to the floor and then drank what remained. Some of them were accompanied by their children who, lying flat on their stomachs, sucked up the trickling liquid with extended lips. This part of the ceremony continued until well after dark. It was followed by feasting, singing and dancing.

Before leaving the gathering – it was eight o'clock, and already a fine drizzle had started to fall through the mist – I exchanged a few words with the diviner, Lephalala. She was delighted the rain had come. It was unusual, she said, for prayers to be answered so soon, and especially before the climax of the ceremony, which, she added, was only due to take place on the following morning. At first light the people would proceed to the nearby burial ground. Some of the goat's blood would then be poured into a shallow furrow to be dug into the ancestral grandfather's grave. Finally, the goat's bones would be placed on this very sacred place, together with a pot of sorghum beer.

The time for tilling and planting was at hand, the diviner concluded. In the months ahead, until the harvests were reaped, the people would work happily together in the lands. Happiest of all would be those who had paid homage to their ancestors not only in spring, midsummer and autumn, but every day throughout the year.

We were drenched by the time we said farewell to the diviner and the patriarch and returned to our truck.

'*Pula! Pula!*' – 'Rain! Rain!' rose a chorus of voices from out of the courtyard as we drove away.

'That is our way of saying thank you when our pleas for rain are answered,' Phoko remarked. 'But tonight it means far more to the worshippers. Tonight they are joyously thankful, and loud in their praise for the ancestral grandfather they so greatly revere.'

The Magical Stick

During the following week, in spite of the cold and rain, we continued to work in the Moletji village. Invited one morning to the home of a headman named Petrus Moloto, we were treated to a display of dancing by a group of women, led by a man blowing a sable antelope horn. Later we were conducted through the headman's settlement, eventually reaching a special hut in which he kept a large assortment of ancestral heirlooms – spears, fighting and walking-sticks, a headrest, stools, skin garments, ornaments, tools and utensils. Great domes of cowdung used as fuel or for building or repairing floors and walls, dotted the area outside the courtyard. At the gateway to his home, pinned to the bottom of a step, was a stick daubed with indigenous medicines. This was a magical stick, the headman explained, and its purpose was to keep out thieves and, in fact, all undesirable visitors. He assured us it had a paralyzing effect on strangers intent on harming himself or his family. Its powers were particularly effective on moonless nights.

Cultural Change

We called on several other dignitaries in the area and shared many hours with them discussing a variety of topics. In this way we were able to assess the extent to which this Kwena tribe had undergone cultural change as a result of contact with White men in neighbouring territories. According to the older people, the most rapid changes had taken place in material things – dress, ornaments, utensils, tools, implements and furniture. Even the Moletji palate had learnt to crave for foods that were foreign to the traditional diet. Less rapid, however, had been the changes in ritual, ceremonies and spiritual attitudes.

The dignitaries we spoke to agreed that change was inevitable and, indeed, essential wherever cultures of differing origins met. As one of them put it: 'We are all travellers along the road of life, but in this kind of travelling there's no time for standing still, unless you don't mind being left behind.

'Even so I'm often disappointed when I look back down that road, and see how some of our traditions have changed. And then I become sad, very sad when I think of others that have fallen along the way, beyond the horizon, never to be seen again.'

But, the dignitary admitted, nothing could stand in the way of change. It was a natural and enduring process as fundamental to life as eating and breathing. Only a dullard would strive to prevent it. Only fools expected rivers to flow suddenly backwards.

Headman Moloto

Opposite   Kopa married woman

THE KOPA

South of Moletji village, just beyond the Strydpoort mountains, the Olifants river flows through a country which is flat in parts and sparsely bushed, but also hilly and lush with subtropical cacti, candelabra euphorbia, indigenous forest and undergrowth. For many centuries the river attracted elephants, lions, leopards and numerous species of antelope. But by the 1800s this haven for game no longer existed. It had become the habitat of Sotho-speaking tribesmen, and was braided with villages, cornfields and cattle posts.

To the west of the Olifants river, about twenty kilometres from the east-bank town of Groblersdal, lies the territory of the Kopa, one of the smallest tribes in the Northern Transvaal. Ruled by a young chief named Boleu II, the Kopa, like the Kwena, have a crocodile totem, and yet culturally they are more closely aligned to the Pedi. Perhaps the most distinctive feature of Kopa culture is their flamboyant mode of dress. In this respect, they resemble neither the people of Moletji nor the Pedi, but seem to have been greatly influenced by the Ndebele. They are renowned for their craftsmanship not only in beadwork but numerous other forms of ornamention.

The most popular ornaments worn by Kopa women are beaded neck, waist and arm hoops similar to those of the Ndebele. These are, however, thinner and lighter than Ndebele hoops, which means that more can be worn at a time. The Kopa also wear aprons, necklaces, metal wristlets and metal ankle bands. On the other hand, instead of shaving their heads, or cropping their hair into patterns as the Ndebele do, they wear headdresses which are as exotic as any to be found south of the Zambezi river.

The Tlopo Headdress

The Kopa headdress (*tlopo*) may not be worn by children. It is a privilege bestowed on adolescent maidens after lengthy seclusion in an initiation lodge. It is fixed permanently on to the crown of the head by highly skilled adult women and takes roughly two hours to complete. So the quality of the finished product depends a great deal on the patience of both craftsman and client.

Before work can begin, the maiden has to wash her hair thoroughly with hot water and soap. It is then rinsed and dried. Next the *tlopo*-maker teases the hair upwards with a thick, metal-toothed comb, simultaneously tugging and patting it into shape, until eventually it stands compactly erect. Then, using scissors, she removes all hair around the ears, the temples and forehead. What remains is an elongated frizzy pear-shaped crest, the narrow part topping the crown and the bulge enveloping the base of the skull.

Once the *tlopo*-maker is satisfied with the shape of the crest, she daubs it thickly with a clay-like substance made of black, finely-ground shale and starch water run off from boiled-up maize. Constantly dipping her fingers into the water, she massages the mixture into the hair, down to the roots. Then she moulds the clay into a solid cap, smoothing it with the blade of a knife. Once the base of the *tlopo* is completed she decorates it with patterns and ornaments.

As a first step she carefully carves a series of lines into the clay, following the outer contours of the headdress, with a nail or piece of sharpened wire. Spaces between the lines are alternately filled in with short, diagonal cuts, diligently neatened with touches of water. A long, thin roll of clay is then thumbed into the *tlopo* to form a ridge down the middle from its tip above the forehead to its bulge at the back. Adorned with beads, metal studs and buttons, the ridge is the most colourful part of the headdress and is of paramount importance to the end result. It varies in appearance according to the imagination of the maker, ideas expressed by the wearer and the variety of baubles used.

While the *tlopo* dries, the scalp around it is shaved with a razor, and smeared with a mixture of red ochre and fat. When completely dry and hard, the headdress itself is wiped down with suet or butter, as protection against the rain. Henceforth it will be worn with pride, especially on ceremonial occasions. Even then, should the weather be bad, it is bound to be wrapped in a head-cloth, for it has to be constantly nursed. The *tlopo* is exceedingly popular as an item of ornamentation, but it has serious disadvantages: it is vulnerable to softening on exposure to rain, and can be easily chipped or cracked.

After marriage, young maidens discard the *tlopo* for a rectangular headdress known as a *motwalo*. For the *tlopo* to be removed it has to be tapped all over with a light, wooden or metal instrument until it disintegrates. When all the fragments have been taken out the hair is washed, dried and then combed backwards and sideways across the head. Then it is clipped into a broad, rectangular pile extending from the forehead to the nape of the neck and is made to stay firmly in position with a pasty fixative of cowdung and ash. It may also be daubed with red ochre, and titivated with beads, but is never patterned with lines, curves or other designs.

Kopa woman

The *motwalo* headdress may not be as attractive as the *tlopo*, but it is just as exotic. Although far less fragile than the *tlopo*, it is still susceptible to damage and is frequently covered with a protective head-cloth. The *motwalo* blends naturally with the hoops that festoon the necks, torsos and limbs of married women and is an outstanding example of African craftsmanship.

Kopa hoops are thinner
and lighter than those
worn by Ndebele women

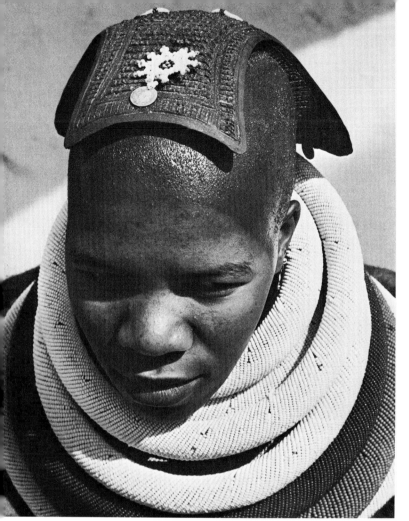

The *tlopo* is fixed permanently to the crown of the head

The back of the *tlopo*. The brass buttons and beads are fixed to clay before it dries

The *motwalo* headdress of married women

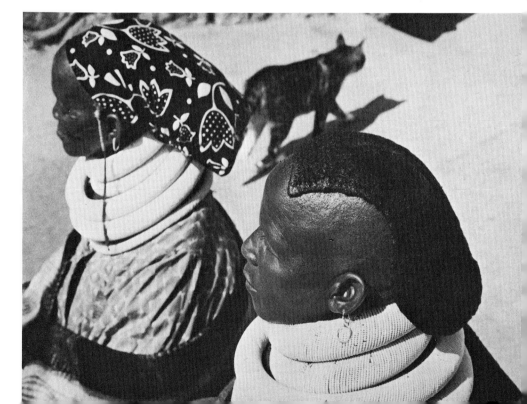

Chief Boleu Rammupudu II

Chieftaincy

I worked among the Kopa on two occasions during the 1960s and began my third visit to this territory on 25 October 1975, the day after my departure with Lionel Friedberg and the camera crew from the Moletji village north of Pietersburg. We arrived in Kopa territory at a most opportune time – the very day on which the young Boleu II was being installed as the new chief of the tribe.

In tribal societies a chief commands the respect of his subjects, if not always their deepest affection. As the symbol of unity in the tribe, he is the pivotal figure around which untold activities revolve. He is at once the ruler and father of the tribe, the supreme judge and preserver of law and order within the territory, the central figure in ritual and ceremony and, finally, the commander-in-chief of his fighting force. He

enjoys a host of privileges, but as a rule is unable to become despotic. This is because tradition precludes him from taking major decisions concerning the tribe unless backed by his councillors.

A chief has a diversity of duties to perform, not least of which is to be readily available to all his subjects, dignitaries and menials alike, should they seek his counsel or have a grievance to voice or merely a favour to ask of him. At all costs he has to be seen as firm and forthright yet understanding; a leader whose wisdom is of the highest order, whose integrity is beyond reproach and whose manner is never undignified.

Among the great majority of southern African tribes, succession to the chieftaincy is by way of a firmly entrenched royal lineage. The reigning chief may be married to more than one wife, and is likely to have several sons. However, usually only the eldest son of the principal wife is recognized as the rightful heir to the throne.

An heir seldom succeeds to the chieftaincy while his father is alive, although there are rare exceptions should the reigning chief become so very old and so very decrepit that he is unable to fulfil his manifold duties. A chief usually rules until removed by death, but the heir is not immediately placed on the throne. This is first occupied by an appointed regent, who undertakes the various functions of the chieftaincy, pending the installation of the legitimate ruler. This period of regency need not last for long, especially if the heir-apparent has attained his majority and has already taken a wife. On the other hand, should he be a child or adolescent at the time of his father's death, it would be considerably prolonged.

When the date for the installation has been fixed, the news spreads rapidly throughout the territory. Early on the morning of the appointed day, a great throng of subjects assembles at the royal village and the proceedings begin. Details of the installation ceremony differ from tribe to tribe, but among peoples of the Northern Transvaal it is customary for a future chief to begin the day by visiting his father's grave. When he returns to the royal village he is loudly hailed by his future subjects. In full view of the gathering, he is first draped by the regent in a leopard-skin mantle and then presented with an assortment of heirlooms – a wooden staff of office, beads and weapons which formerly belonged to the ancestral chiefs of his lineage.

Lengthy speeches are now delivered by various dignitaries. The new chief is reminded of the virtues of his predecessors, the responsibilities that await him in his role as

Manala women wearing
maphoto aprons, seated in
the courtyard of a
homestead

Above The crocodile totem of Chief Boleu II

The dancers gather around the drummer

Leader of the dance

Motwalo headdresses
wrapped in cloth and
topped with artificial
flowers, ribbons and
ostrich feathers

a chief and the need to blend his own brand of wisdom with that of the councillors. He is also extolled, given assurances of loyalty and encouraged to view the future with confidence. Finally, he himself addresses the throng, pledging to serve the tribe unstintingly. He is constantly interrupted with exclamations of praise, and ends his speech amidst thunderous acclaim. This marks the end of the installation and the start of many hours of festivity.

The *mosate* or royal village of Boleu II is situated in the heart of the Tafelkop district, north-west of Groblersdal. It consists of the chief's modern European-style home, a number of outhouses, enclosures for cattle, sheep and goats and an arena where gatherings are held. Fronted with courtyards and mud-plastered walls, it looks on to a gateway over which two crocodiles, cut from metal plating, face each other in the form of an arch. Beyond the gateway, the landscape gradually unfolds in a succession of valleys and hills, a vast panorama speckled with anthills and dotted with tribal homesteads, cattlefolds and clusters of bush.

It was past noon when we reached the royal village. Boleu II had just been installed as chief of the Kopa tribe, and had retired with his retinue and guests to a marquee tent for lunch. The *mosate* swarmed with people, and the air was filled with the sound of happy conversation, singing, laughter and the beating of drums. It also suddenly resounded to an explosion of thunder as low-lying clouds, rolling in from the east, quickly spread over Tafelkop.

A cry went up from the crowd – '*Pula! Pula!* – Rain! Rain!' Rain, symbolic of fertility and impending good fortune – a wonderful omen on a day such as this. So, although unsheltered, the people rejoiced. And when the rain came down, they began to cheer and to clap their hands; many of the younger folk stripped to the waist.

The storm did not last for long. The noisy ceiling of clouds moved on to the west leaving a misty drizzle in its wake. The crowd grew silent as from the arena came the blare of *phalaphala* trumpets (made from sable antelope horns), the piping of flutes and the ear-piercing skirl of metal whistles. This signalled the start of the dancing and instinctively the crowd moved backwards, forming a compact ring around the arena. Next moment, a long line of women moved into the space, and encircling the central part began dancing to the rhythm of a drum.

They were magnificently attired in Kopa finery – their necks, shoulders, waists and arms profusely adorned with beaded hoops, and their ankles with copper and wire rings or rattles made of moth cocoons. Their *motwalo* headdresses were wrapped in gaudy cloths, most of which were topped with flowers, ribbons and ostrich feathers. They also carried painted walking sticks, knobkerries, shepherds' crooks, furled umbrellas and the lids of metal cooking pots. One of them bore a platter of palm leaves on her head, on the top of which lay an open-mouthed crocodile skilfully carved from wood.

The women danced gracefully to the slow, monotonous boom of the drum, stamping their feet with the precision of a platoon of soldiers marking time. Backs erect and heads held high, they raised their arms, now sideways, now forward, their torsos simultaneously swaying to the left and right. This dance, like those they were later to perform in Chief Boleu's courtyard, was not as animated as others I had previously witnessed in the Northern Transvaal. Its real fascination stemmed from the dignified bearing of the women, the nostalgic and somewhat mournful songs they sang quietly in perfect harmony and the heavy thud of their feet in accord with the drum.

The dancing continued until darkness crept over Tafelkop. Chief Boleu's *mosate* resounded to myriad voices as the crowd moved into the arena where fires had been lit and food brought in for a feast. Soon an aroma of roasting meat hung over the village, and the people rejoiced, singing, dancing or chatting in groups. As we walked through the arena, thankful that the festivity could take place unhindered by rain, we were amazed at the number of guests who bewailed the departure of the afternoon's storm.

The rain had come suddenly and had then disappeared...so little, and yet more than enough. *Pula!* – Rain! Prime sustainer of life, symbol of prosperity and happiness...Boleu II had been truly blessed!

Venda

For a while I found it puzzling that Mzilikazi never brought the Venda tribes into the Matabele fold, even though his settlement, The Place of Rest, was no more than a week's march from Venda. Why should they have been spared while their neighbours were decimated? Had they won his favour in some peculiar way; did he fear their magical practices; or had they merely convinced him that as mountain-dwellers they were too insignificant to warrant subjugation? With these queries in mind, I decided to visit the Venda in 1960 and seek an interview with at least one of their chroniclers. I had come to regard this trip as a matter of urgency, even though I realized my findings might contribute no more than a paragraph or two to Mzilikazi's biography.

Venda, the most northerly tribal complex in the Transvaal, lies between the Limpopo and Letaba rivers, and roughly between Louis Trichardt in the west and the Kruger National Park in the east. Traversed by the Soutpansberg range – a staccato of loping mountains, spurs, krantzes, valleys and chasms, it is always hot in summer, rarely intensely cold in winter and often prone to bothersome winds. North of the mountains the territory is sun-bitten, arid and stubbled with scrub, thornbush and gigantic baobab trees. This part of the territory is thinly populated. In the south, where the rainfall is relatively high, the land is grassy and afforested and watered by two major rivers, the Mutale and Luvuvhu, as well as numerous tributaries and hill-slope springs. Here most of the villages, grain fields and pastures are situated. It is the most densely populated area in Venda.

According to legend, the land of the Venda was virtually uninhabited until the end of the seventeenth century, apart from a sprinkling of nomadic Bushmen hunterfolk and little colonies of African tribesmen known as Ngona. Then, in the early 1700s, following an outbreak of factional feuding in Karanga territory north of the Limpopo river, hordes of fugitives headed by their chiefs migrated southwards. Crossing the arid regions beyond the river and then the Soutpansberg range, they spread out and regrouped with their chiefs into twenty-six tiny tribes. These fugitives were the pioneer Venda of the Northern Transvaal, a people who, although closely linked with the Karanga tribes, were destined to develop a distinctive identity in the course of time.

By the middle of the nineteenth century, not only the culture of the Venda but also their language had undergone considerable change. This was due largely to their self-imposed isolation in the natural fastnesses of the

Northern Venda is arid and punctuated with
gigantic baobab trees

Soutpansberg mountains, as well as to the fact that, in their
southward flight, they had been accompanied by groups of
Lemba. A people of Negro and Arab descent, the Lemba
were master craftsmen, astute entrepreneurs and psychic
practitioners of the highest order.

Venda Chronicler

I arrived in Venda during the afternoon of the last Monday in
August 1960. The country was parched after a rainless
winter, and the villages, trees and pastures were tinctured
with vermillion dust deposited by recent winds. Having
pitched camp among the bushes on the outskirts of Sibasa,

the capital town, I made arrangements with a local dignitary
called Mulaudzi to be taken to Chief Nelwamondo. I had
been told the chief was one of the outstanding chroniclers of
Venda and that his village was situated in the hills not far to
the west.

Mulaudzi and I set out by truck for Nelwamondo's place
on the Tuesday morning. We followed a dusty track through
a bushy valley, eventually drawing up at its western extremity
near a trading store. I gathered my cameras and tape recorder,
and we trudged up a winding footpath into the slopes of a
nearby hill. After about an hour's climb, we reached the
summit and, brushing our way through a thicket of mimosa,
mopani, white stinkwood and buffalo thorn, we came
suddenly upon the palisades of Nelwamondo's village.
Farther on, at the gateway, we paused to rest and wipe our
sweating faces. Looking around me I noticed the village was
concealed among the rocks and indigenous forest. I realized
now why I had not been able to see it from the valley, even
with the aid of binoculars.

We were met at the gateway by a councillor who led us first
through the village *khoro*, then along a passage flanked by tall
reed-hedges and finally across a clay-floored clearing to Chief
Nelwamondo's three whitewashed rondavel homes.
Ushering us to a circle of homemade benches in the shade of a
marulla tree, the councillor told us to be seated while he
reported our presence to the chief. He returned soon
afterwards with Nelwamondo.

The chief, I guessed, studying his features, was about sixty-
five years old. Tall and wiry, he was dressed in a black jacket,
a white open-neck shirt, black trousers and boots and a long-
peaked military cap. He had deep-set eyes, a furrowed
forehead, greying temples and lips that curled into a generous
smile the moment he saw us. He was the kind of man who,
although tautly sinewed with age and toughened by the
rigours of an outdoor life, looked happily at peace with the
world around him. The kind of man one feels instantly
pleased to meet and determined to keep as a friend. As things
turned out, I was to find him an outstanding informant on
Venda history and culture.

When he learned I was writing Mzilikazi's biography, and
had followed the conqueror's trail through southern Africa,
Chief Nelwamondo said he was surprised I had not visited
Venda before. Had I omitted the Venda from my itinerary, he
asked, on the assumption that because they were the smallest
tribal group in the Northern Transvaal, they had been
deliberately by-passed by the warlike Matabele? Did I not

A veteran Zulu
regimental commander.
abaKwaZulu warriors of
this calibre took part in
the subjugation of the
inland tribes

The author's camp on the outskirts of Sibasa. A
slaughtered goat is being skinned in preparation
for the evening meal

know that, because of their uncommon skill in smelting iron
ore and in forging assegai and hoe blades, Mzilikazi had
earmarked the Venda for incorporation in his growing tribe?
Mzilikazi had, in fact, regarded the Venda as culturally
superior to the Pedi and other neighbouring tribes. He had
actually attempted to conquer them, but on failing to do so
had decided instead to court their friendship. Was this not
extraordinary; was it not a tribute to the Venda that although
a relatively defenceless people, they had escaped Mzilikazi's
wrath, continuing to live in peace while other tribes were
being attacked and subjugated?

'Whenever I think of Mzilikazi,' said the chief, 'I see him as
a young, black warrior who was cunning like a jackal and
strong as a lion, and I feel a pride within me – proud to be
black like he was. Perhaps, had he conquered the Venda, as
he conquered the Pedi and other tribes, I would have grown
up judging him differently. I would have acknowledged his
strength but questioned his courage, condemned his cunning
and disputed his wisdom. It is difficult to admire a man who
has caused you harm, and impossible to consider him wise. So
my thoughts of Mzilikazi are unprejudiced. I tell myself he

was gifted not only with the qualities I have already
mentioned, but also with such uncommon vision that he was
able to found the Matabele dynasty, and become just as
powerful as King Shaka of the Zulu had been.

'Now you have asked my opinion on why the Venda were
spared by the Matabele when other tribes were not,' the chief
continued. 'Well,' he smiled, 'I doubt if anyone can answer
this question with certainty, especially as there are chroniclers
who maintain that Mzilikazi's armies never reached this far.
Nonsense, I say, that's nonsense! There is no doubt in my
mind that the Matabele did march on Venda – this must have
been shortly after their defeat of the Pedi – and that they fully
intended conquering our forefathers as had been their
practice everywhere else. But now we must ask ourselves
why they failed. Was it because they found the Venda too
powerful to conquer? No, the Venda were not a warlike
people. Was it because they took pity on them? No. So, then
what could have caused them to fail?'

'Perhaps they found the country too mountainous and
bushy and hot,' I felt obliged to suggest.

'That's right,' he exclaimed, 'but that wasn't all. It's true
they found that Venda villages were built high up in the
mountains like mine, most of them hidden by bush. This
meant the Matabele had to do much climbing and searching
and wasting time, only to discover on reaching a village that
the Venda had very few cattle because of the tsetse fly. They
also found that the Venda were so few in number and so
widely scattered that a whole day could pass without their
finding a village or even a person worth robbing. It meant
much had to be done for very little reward, and the Matabele
were accustomed to just the opposite.

'There was also the constant danger of attack by lions,
leopards, elephants and buffalo. You see, Venda then was not
as it is now. It swarmed with game, which was a good thing
except, as I have already said, some of the animals were so
wild and fierce that they often spread terror in the villages,
and made strangers in particular feel unwelcome. And the
snakes! Mambas, pythons, cobras, puffadders and many
other kinds. It is said that several Matabele were bitten by
snakes and, dying in pain, their death-shrieks echoed through
the mountains causing their fellow-marauders to move
cautiously by day and to sleep very shakily at nights.

'For these various reasons and others, the Matabele were
soon to look upon Venda as an undesirable place. On the
other hand, they are said to have been kindly treated by our
people, receiving gifts of newly cooked food and baskets of

Children of the same age play together in groups

grain for the journey ahead. No, Venda was not the kind of territory the invaders had hoped it would be. It was a place they needed to visit, if only to realize it need not be visited again.'

'Did this mean that the Venda had no further dealings with the Matabele?' I asked.

'Oh no,' the chief replied, 'it only meant that the invaders decided there were better places to invade. And in meeting some of our chiefs of that time, they came to an agreement with them: provided the Venda sent regular tribute of hoe and assegai blades to Mzilikazi's military village on the Aapies river, they would be left in peace. It was a good arrangement, especially for the people of Venda.'

While we talked beneath the *marulla* tree, its shadow had been furtively receding, and we found ourselves exposed to the stabbing rays of the morning sun. Moving our benches back into the shade, we exchanged tobacco pouches and lit our pipes.

'Are you staying long in Venda?' asked Nelwamondo.

'No,' I replied, 'I must leave on Friday.'

'On Friday!' he exclaimed in astonishment.

'Yes,' I said, 'but I will come back soon.'

'Then come towards the end of September,' retorted the chief, 'because by then the *domba* will be at its best.'

The *domba* – the most important and spectacular initiation ceremony for Venda maidens – this I would not miss at any cost.

The chief left us and for the next three hours I was shown through the village by the councillor and Mulaudzi, my guide. In the gathering place my attention was drawn to the central part, where cords of smoke snaked lazily upwards from a pile of smouldering logs. This, the councillor explained, was where the initiates danced during the *domba* ceremony. As they had begun dancing at dawn, continuing until after sunrise, they were now resting and eating in a special hut. Later they would be summoned by their overseer and given chores to do.

The chief's cattlefold was situated to the right of us, and beside it was an enclosure for calves. The entire gathering place was encircled by a palisade of sharpened stakes. Further embraced by bush and trees, it was shadowy, cool and cut off from the prevailing hilltop winds.

We crossed the gathering place and, reaching the rear of the cattlefold, followed a pathway into the central part of the village. On either side of us was a procession of courtyards,

rondavel huts and conical-roofed granaries. We passed groups of children noisily at play, groups of women laboriously grinding, stamping or winnowing grain and groups of men leisurely chatting over a pot of home-brewed beer.

On the farthest side of the village were the communal threshing floors. Covered with husks and maize cobs, they had attracted a multitude of birds – sparrows, doves, finches, starlings and crows, which burst into flight as we came into view. At the rear of the homesteads where the ash and rubbish heaps are situated, the villagers' fowls, ducks, geese and pigs were foraging for porridge-pot scrapings, stew bones and the residue of recently sifted beer. Our presence was constantly being challenged by dogs, and we were suspiciously watched by countless cats. These cats glared down at us from courtyard walls, the eaves of huts or the roofs of granaries. They were rotund from over-eating, for the village was infested with rats and mice.

Returning to the chief's section of the village, we came upon a spacious shelter used specifically for stamping grain. It consisted of a thatched roof supported on planted poles and a plastered floor into which eight wooden stamping blocks had been sunk. Within it was a nook made of planking where pestles, baskets, winnowing trays, earthen pots and calabash scoops were kept. There was also a hearth where the workers made wood or cowdung fires on wintry days.

Adjoining this shelter was a small sleeping hut (*khombo*), where visiting bachelors were accommodated. Beside it, within a palisaded courtyard, was a larger one, the *tshivambo*, for housing prominent guests. This part of the village, I noticed, was in perfect repair. Indeed the entire royal village was among the neatest I had seen in southern Africa.

The Terraced Village

We left Chief Nelwamondo's place late in the afternoon, arriving back in camp after sundown. Next morning, Mulaudzi and I set out for the royal village of Vhavenda Vho-Tshisevhe Netshimbupfe, one of Venda's best-known chiefs.

As the district over which Netshimbupfe rules lies well to the south of the territory's entanglement of mountain ranges, we travelled through countryside now flat and bushy, now overspread with grasslands and now studded with densely wooded hills. We crossed only one small river, the Luvuvhu. Upstream, its edges were lined with women, some washing

Opposite   A group of women bound for the
threshing floor

The top terrace of Chief Netshimbupfe's village

bundles of clothing and others scooping water into pots or buckets for use in nearby villages. The pools downstream swarmed with cattle and goats, the sedges with cattle egrets and the rocks with herdboys and dogs.

We caught sight of Chief Netshimbupfe's village long before reaching it. Built on terraces carved into the northern face of a hillock, it stood out clearly in the morning sun against a compact background of thornbush and indigenous trees. We drew up at the foot of the settlement close to the *khoro* or gathering place. Unlike Chief Nelwamondo's *khoro* and others I was later to visit, this one was not enclosed with palisades. It consisted merely of a clump of trees, a fireplace and a circle of benches.

We had just stepped out of the truck when a councillor, recognizing Mulaudzi, hailed us from the topmost terrace of the village. He came hurrying down the slope and, reaching the *khoro*, led us to the ring of benches. We then sat down together, and discussed the reason for my visit to Venda and especially to Netshimbupfe's place. The chief, he said, was about to depart for Sibasa, and might not agree to our presence in the village during his absence. He suggested we come back some other time, but on Mulaudzi's insistence agreed to confer with the chief and find out which day would suit him best. Leaving us in the shade of the trees, he retraced his steps up the slope. He rejoined us about twenty minutes later with news that Netshimbupfe wanted to see us before he left.

The climb into the village, laden with equipment, was not as arduous as I had expected. This was because the path zigzagged widely across the slope, counteracting the steep gradients between each of the terraces.

On the various terraces were family homesteads, plastered courtyards and encircling walls built either of clay or stone. Whereas in Chief Nelwamondo's village most of the homes were cylindrical in shape, here they were predominantly rectangular. They were also larger, the thatched roofs extending so far beyond the walls that the eaves had had to be supported on poles. This added a verandah to each of the sides. I noticed, as we continued up the slope, that the people made use of their verandahs not only for protection against the sun, but also as storage places for pots, baskets, drums, mats and agricultural implements.

We met Chief Netshimbupfe near the highest point of the village. Short and chubby, he was immaculately dressed in a brown tweed jacket and flannel trousers with tie and hat to match. He wore a trimmed moustache, and a hint of beard

Chief Vhavenda Vho-Tshisevhe Netshimbupfe

immediately beneath his lower lip. He was a genial man with a hearty laugh and constantly smiling eyes and mouth. He was obviously also a patient man, for despite the inconvenience he had been caused by our untimely arrival, he showed not the slightest sign of displeasure. After fifteen minutes together, he glanced at his watch, and declared apologetically that he had to leave us. The councillor and Mulaudzi, he said, could take me to all parts of the village, and show me whatever I wished to see.

After the chief had left us, as we moved down the slope from terrace to terrace, I soon realized that this royal village was more elaborate than the one we had visited the day before. For example, virtually all the homes, including the cylindrical ones, were larger; the granaries were more numerous and the threshing floors more spacious. Moreover, because of its vulnerability to washaways in the rainy season, the site had been provided with a comparatively intricate system of protective walls. Some of these were small, narrow and made of clay, designed to steer rushing water away from the homesteads. Others were tall and thick and made of stone; they supported the terraces to prevent their coming apart. I found two additional features of the village of particular interest – a brewery for indigenous beer and a pottery which, according to Mulaudzi, was the finest of its kind in the territory.

A Venda Brewery

Beer is brewed in Venda, as in all tribal societies, throughout the year. A home without beer, I have heard it said, is like a spring without water. Just as there cannot be life without water, so a tribe cannot live without beer. It cultivates friendships, encourages hospitality and, if taken in moderation, harnesses anger at times of dissension. It is offered to visitors, be they relatives, friends, acquaintances or strangers, and is always in ready supply on festive and ceremonial occasions. Beer is particularly popular during the planting and reaping seasons when people work together in groups. It is also the form of tribute most commonly received by chiefs and headmen from subjects, and the offering most consistently dedicated to ancestral spirits. Finally, beer is regarded not only as a beverage but also a food. Made of sorghum, maize or finger millet (*eleusine*), it is highly nutritious, and rich in roughage. It has a low alcohol content, and is therefore drunk more frequently and in larger quantities than such potent brews as are made from *marulla* fruit or the sap of the *isundu* and *ilala* palm. Indigenous beer is a palatable drink, and by virtue of its slightly sour taste is outstanding for quenching thirst, especially in subtropical regions like Venda.

Netshimbupfe's brewery consisted of a thatched rectangular hut the floors and walls of which were plastered with clay, and the interior lined on every side with the biggest beerpots to be found in southern Africa. Sunk halfway into the floor of the hut, these earthen pots are thick and durable and extremely heavy. About one metre in diameter, they each hold on average no less than 150 litres of beer.

When we entered the building, the pots were full to the brim with beer in various stages of maturity. In some of them, it was ready for drinking, and in others it was still in the throes of fermentation and was therefore frothy and effervescent. Seated beside a pot was one of the village brewers who, seeing us approach, reached for a calabash scoop which she filled with beer for the councillor to sample. By the way he smacked his lips in anticipation, I knew she had reason to be proud of her handiwork.

Having emptied the scoop in a single breath, again smacking his lips, the councillor returned the scoop to the brewer. Now Mulaudzi and I were given a turn. It was excellent beer. I thought of the occasions I had seen this popular beverage being made in other tribal territories, so I asked the brewer briefly to describe the method she used.

'We are at present using sorghum,' she said, 'which must first be threshed and then soaked in water for two full days. After this, the water is poured away, and the grain spread out and covered with mats to keep it moist. Within the next day or two, depending on the time of year, the grain will have started to shoot; so it is opened up and exposed to the sun until it has dried. Now the sorghum is collected, stamped into meal, poured into pots and boiled in water from, say, the morning until late afternoon. Then it is left to cool.

'I have forgotten to mention,' the brewer continued, 'that not all the germinated grain is stamped into meal. Some of it has to be kept apart, and then added to the cooling beer to make it ferment.

'The fermenting, by the way, must be allowed to continue for at least a day, after which the beer is ready. Almost, that is, because it has still to be poured through a sieve to remove the husks.'

'And all the time it is kept very cool,' added the councillor, wiping his brow.

'Very cool,' said the brewer, 'because the cooler it is, the nicer it tastes, and the better it will be for quenching thirst.

'So this is how we make our beer,' she concluded, 'just as we have been taught by our mothers. All women can make it, and make it well, knowing that a home must always have it. Not too much at a time; just enough for the needs of the family.'

'Not too much at a time?' cried the councillor, feigning surprise. 'Then what about all this beer you're brewing now?'

'It's another matter when you're brewing for a chief,' she replied. 'Because it's not only his family you're thinking of. You must remember he is seldom without visitors; and when important celebrities arrive and ceremonies take place, it is he who is expected to provide the beer.'

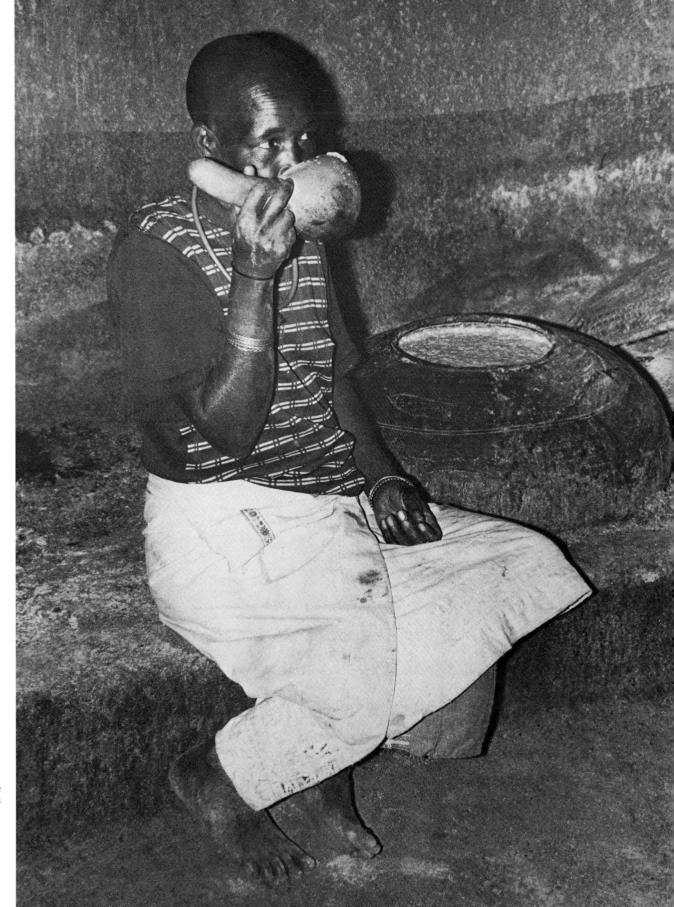

The brewer beside one
of the sunken beerpots
within the village
brewery

Royal Matriarch

After a second round from the calabash scoop we left the brewery and retraced our steps towards the bottom of the village. On one of the lower terraces we were told by the councillor to wait at a courtyard gate until invited to enter. We were at the home of Chief Netshimbupfe's mother – MaVhavenda Vho-Tshisevhe.

I could see her seated on a mat in the shade of one of the courtyard walls. About fifty-five years old, MaVhavenda was dressed in a skirt and cloak made of blue, striped cloth, and wore wire bracelets, wire anklets, a string of beads and tiny brass earrings. Matriarch of the village, she was surrounded by a group of women, all of them roughly the same age as herself. They were busy with beadwork, including MaVhavenda, and chatted in muted tones.

Mulaudzi had told me about MaVhavenda during the morning and, although eager to meet her, I had not dared suggest we should visit her home. I was convinced she would not want to see me, especially as it was not customary for village males, let alone strangers, to be admitted to the quarters of female royalty. I was therefore both surprised and delighted when I found myself outside her home.

Not long after our arrival, MaVhavenda beckoned us to enter the courtyard and, greeting us with a nod of the head, sent a maiden to fetch us a bench. Observing my cameras, she asked if I had been taking photographs.

'Many,' I said, adding I was grateful for the cooperation I had received in the village.

'Do you intend taking more?' she continued.

'I would like to,' I replied.

'What of?' she queried.

'Well,' I said, thinking fast, 'we are on our way to the pottery on the other side of the *khoro*, and I'm sure there will be much of interest there.'

'What else?' she insisted.

I paused, crossing my fingers.

'I should very much like to photograph you.'

'Me!' she exclaimed. 'You want to photograph me?'

'Only if it would please you,' I croaked, fearing I might have offended her.

'It would indeed make me pleased,' she said smiling now, 'especially as it seems you will also be pleased.'

Queen Mother MaVhavenda

MaVhavenda in the courtyard of her home

I gave a sigh of relief, much to the amusement of the councillor, Mulaudzi and the group of women. I learned later that MaVhavenda had wanted her photograph taken the moment she caught sight of me at the courtyard gate. She had actually been afraid I might pass her by.

I took several portrait shots of MaVhavenda in her home and she then returned to her companions and sat down among them. This gave me an opportunity to move discreetly about the courtyard, and to capture her in a variety of unposed attitudes. After twenty minutes or more, I packed my cameras, bade her farewell and set out for the pottery with Mulaudzi and the councillor.

The Pottery

The Venda are without doubt the most accomplished tribal potters south of the Limpopo river. Much of their skill can be attributed to the influence of the Lemba who accompanied them to the south in the 1700s. The Lemba were exceptional craftsmen, who excelled not only in pot-making but also in iron work, carving, weaving and beadwork. They were generally accepted by the Venda as advisers and tutors.

Pottery in Venda, as in other tribal territories, is a female occupation and ranks as the most demanding of traditional crafts. It is pursued by select groups of women who, apart from the apprenticeship they have had to serve, are specially gifted with patience and, above all, a keen eye for symmetry. The potter's wheel is unknown to them, so that the shapes of their pots tend to be stereotyped. But despite this, the standard of workmanship can hardly be faulted. Venda pots are beautiful.

We found the village pottery in a clearing among the thorntrees. It consisted of three shallow firing pits which served as kilns, a mound of clay, another of sand and scores of pots arranged in lots according to size.

There were five women at work in the pottery, among them the councillor's eldest daughter. Carrying an infant on her back, she was examining a range of newly baked beer pots as we arrived. She was about twenty-five years old and, according to her father, a devoted potter. When I asked her to explain how she made her pots, she agreed reluctantly, adding that her four companions were more skilled than she.

'This is the clay we use,' she began, pointing to one of the mounds. 'It is fetched from the river, and although usually quite clean and smooth, it has to be pounded with a pole to make it fine. We then take out all the pebbles, roots, grass and pieces of stick; in fact, everything hard that will make our pots uneven or cause them to crack.

'When the clay is ready we mix it with water to make it soft, adding sifted sand, not much, but enough for the pots to be extra strong.

'We begin making a pot by taking a chunk of the clay we have softened, and flattening it into the shape of a circle. Then, taking more clay, not too much at a time, we roll it into strips between the palms of our hands. We keep on doing this, first winding the strips around the base of the pot, and then carefully one on top of the other. And, as the bottom of the pot starts taking shape, we start to use our thumbs, joining and smoothing the inside of the strips, our fingers preventing the outside from coming apart.

Venda pots – from smallest to biggest

'When the pot is about as high as an up-pointed hand, growing wider strip after strip, we make use of a piece of broken pot, pressing it lightly against the inside to keep the clay properly in place. Most of the work is now done with the hand that is free: adding bits of clay, packing these against the piece of broken pot, and then smoothing inside and outside with very wet fingers or a piece of goat-skin which we keep dipping in water. The smaller pots are easiest to make, but the big ones, the beer-pots, give plenty of trouble being wide and high and so very heavy.

'But working here is not really difficult. It is the young girls that always have something to complain about. The older women are different, being so used to pot-making that they can talk to each other while working, sometimes not looking at what they are doing, but knowing their hands will not make mistakes.

The pottery at Chief Netshimbupfe's village.

'The finished pots are decorated with lines and dots, and this we do with a nail or knife or sharpened wire. The older women also use long, white thorns which they pick from the bushes close to the pottery. After decorating the pots must be left to dry in the sun for three or four days. Then they are packed in the firing pits and baked for a further day. The fire must never become too big, because the clay will crack; so we keep it burning slowly around the pots. This is a pleasure in winter when the days are cold, but not so pleasant at this time of the year when you want to be out of the sun and in the shade of the trees.

'Newly baked pots are always black from the soot and smoke, and never look nice at first. So as soon as they have cooled, we rub them down with a piece of skin, using the soot as a polish. This makes them shine, and by the time we have finished they look beautiful.'

The potter's baby had begun to whimper, so she lifted it out of the goat-skin sling in which it had been sitting astride her back and held it lovingly against her breast. As we left her, she was swaying gently leftwards and rightwards and softly humming a lullaby.

The lower section of the *khoro* at the Mukumbani
royal village

The Royal Conservationist

It was already dark when Mulaudzi and I set out for our camp
near Sibasa. We lit a fire, unpacked the truck and made our
beds on a canvas spread out beneath the trees. After an
inadequate wash – we had little water in camp and were
covered with dust from head to toe – we sat down to a meal of
canned beef and assorted vegetables, canned apricots, biscuits and coffee. The night was hot, so we let the fire burn out
and, in the light of a hurricane lamp, discussed the events of
the day. But Mulaudzi began to yawn and stretch and blink
his eyes, complaining they were sore and refused to stay open.
When I suggested he should go to bed he readily agreed. He
curled himself under a blanket and immediately drifted into a
snory sleep. I remained at the fireside. I replayed the tape
recordings I had made during the day, and then brought my

diary up to date. It was past midnight when I joined Mulaudzi.

Daybreak in an African bushveld is an uplifting experience, accompanied by a miscellany of insect, bird and animal sound, myriad tints and hues and air so fresh as to make one glad of the gift of breathing. Daybreak in Venda begins with the frantic crowing of village roosters, the yapping of dogs, the bellowing of cattle, the tantalizing buzz of blow-fly, bees and beetles and the ear-rending cacophony of francolins. It is a time for jumping out of bed, lighting the fire and offering a toast to the rising sun with a mug of steaming coffee.

Mulaudzi and I were up and dressed by the first light of dawn. I was busy lighting my pipe, waiting for the coffee pot to come to the boil, when a Venda messenger arrived in camp. To my surprise, he told us he had made arrangements for us to visit the territory of Chief Ratshalinga Tshivhase, north of Sibasa.

'That's good,' cried Mulaudzi, turning to me, 'you'll like it there. I sent this man two days ago to ask the chief if we could see him. I decided not to tell you in case he refused and you were disappointed.

'Did you speak to the chief?' Mulaudzi asked the messenger.

'He was away in Louis Trichardt,' the man replied, 'so I spoke to the councillors.'

'And then?'

'Well, they decided you should go to the Mukumbani royal village, where you'd be given a guide to show you around.'

'Mukumbani,' said Mulaudzi, turning again to me, 'is the village of the chief's predecessor, Chief Phiriphiri Tshivashe. It is one of the oldest royal villages in Venda, and one of the best to see.'

After a hasty breakfast, we set out northwards through the valleys and hills. Mulaudzi, sitting beside me, had become suddenly pensive. As he seemed reluctant to talk I confined my comments to the beauty of the countryside, to complaining about the gathering heat and to lamenting the refusal of the heavens to bring forth rain. Then, as if awakening from a dream, he sat up straight, yawned loudly and said: 'Chief Phiriphiri and I were very good friends, right up to the time of his death in 1952.'

'How long did he rule?' I asked, 'and what was he like?'

'He was placed on the Tshivashe throne in 1932,' continued Mulaudzi, 'and was very popular except among certain people who found him much too hot-headed, and quarrelled with him. The chief as I knew him was a very kind man, and yet so strict that many of his subjects kept out of his way. For although he did much to help his followers and make them happy, he also severely punished those who broke the law, or treated their families unkindly or were disrespectful to their superiors. His followers grew accustomed to orderliness, which meant they were spared the unhappiness that unruly people so frequently suffer. It was not that Phiriphiri's subjects were very different to other Venda people, but he was stricter than most other chiefs. However, I am specially praising Chief Phiriphiri for a very good reason: he was my chief, and his royal village, Mukumbani, is where I was born, where I grew up and where my old father and other relatives are still living today.'

Mulaudzi went on to tell me, among other things, that the chief had had an uncommon love for birds and wild animals, and had spent much of his time in the wooded hill-slopes above his village, in order to watch and admire them.

'It is usual for Venda men to love their cattle, goats and sheep,' Mulaudzi said, 'but you don't see every day the kind of love the chief had for animals, all animals that is.

'Many years ago, for instance, a leopard visited his goat pen, stealing one of his goats and devouring all but its hind quarters in the bush near by. Instead of having it hunted down and killed, he had what was left of the carcass taken into the hills for other leopards to eat. Even the baboons that raided his lands were sometimes sent grain and pumpkins, as if they deserved to be rewarded. And the vultures! The chief loved vultures, and from time to time would have an old or injured ox slaughtered, and its carcass taken to a place where he could watch those huge birds feed.

'One day – this I will never forget – I was sitting with the chief and some of his councillors in the courtyard of his home. It was a cloudless afternoon, and we saw a great circle of vultures, many hundreds of them, floating round and round towards us across the hills. Suddenly the chief jumped to his feet, flung his arms above his head, his fingers outstretched, and cried out excitedly, over and over: "Look at them, are they not beautiful? Look how smoothly they fly! Ah, look at them. Those are my very own birds!"'

Mulaudzi burst into laughter and, leaning forward, covered his face with his hands.

'What do you find so funny?' I asked.

'Those birds,' he cried, his cheeks moist with the tears of laughter, 'those ugly birds. How could anyone find them so beautiful?'

INITIATION FOR GIRLS

The Vhusha Lodge

We had been travelling for just on an hour when the road, veering sharply upwards into the face of a hill, cut through an avenue of trees and bush and ivory palms. The slopes above us were densely wooded and interspersed with homesteads, only the rooftops peeping occasionally out of the foliage. Below, the woods were not as dense, so the homesteads appeared to be far more numerous. Farther down the slopes fanned into a valley, much of it patched with untilled maize and sorghum fields.

As we came to the end of the avenue, we entered Mukumbani, the late Chief Phiriphiri's village. Built on terraces in much the same way as Chief Netshimbupfe's place, it was to a great extent obscured by gigantic trees and clumps of banana palm. In the foreground was a vast arena, and within it the khoro or gathering place. The entire area was hedged with a wall of loosely-packed stones.

Mulaudzi and I were met in the khoro by a councillor named Ramalonga, who asked me what aspect of Venda culture I had come to study. I replied that I was particularly keen to learn about the initiation of boys and girls, adding I would be attending the domba ceremony at Chief Nelwamondo's village towards the end of September.

'That's good,' he said, 'because the domba is not being held in our village this year. And in any case, before you attend the domba, you should attend the vhusha, and this we can show you here.'

Looking over his shoulder, the councillor noticed a woman crossing the arena with a pot of beer on her head. So he called out to her to go to the vhusha lodge, and inform the overseers of our impending visit. The three of us lit our pipes, exchanged pinches of snuff and shared a pot of beer. We talked about the weather, the harvests of previous years and the tilling, planting and other activities that awaited the arrival of the summer rains. After about an hour, a maiden arrived with news that the overseers were ready to receive us.

We followed the maiden across the arena and, reaching a gateway in the stone wall, entered a courtyard in which was a solitary rondavel hut. It was immense – at least four times larger than the family huts of similar shape I had so far seen in Venda. It had two doorways which faced each other across the centre, and a roof that extended so far beyond its walls that the thatch almost reached the courtyard floor. Within its shadowy interior, seated side by side against the wall, were ten young girls. Heads bowed and arms folded, they were naked except for the tiny apron worn by female initiates. These were the vhusha girls.

The vhusha is a six-day ceremony which is arranged for girls soon after their first menstruation. For with the arrival of menses childhood is seen as having come to an end, and adolescence officially begun. Ahead lies the road to adulthood, and as a first step the future wives and mothers of the tribe need to be initiated into forsaking childish practices, and adopting a more responsible attitude to life. They are therefore taken into the seclusion of a lodge, where they are strictly superintended by chosen overseers and given regular instruction on a variety of subjects.

Vhusha girls are taught that humility is the essence of Venda womanhood. During their stay in the lodge, they have to assume a bearing of abject subservience – heads bowed, shoulders stooped and arms folded or hands cupped beneath the chin. They are also made to perform menial tasks such as carrying heavy stones from one side of the lodge to the other, or bearing weighted loads on their backs or heads. They may be made to crawl around the courtyard, or to wriggle on their stomachs like snakes within the vhusha hut, or to hold glowing embers in their fingers or the palms of their hands. These various tasks are perceived by the overseers as having a humbling effect on initiates.

Although the instruction received by the girls covers a wide spectrum of Venda life it is devoted mainly to impending betrothal, marriage and sexual behaviour. The girls are warned against flirtations with irresponsible youths, and constantly reminded that, just as decaying offal attracts flies and cockroaches, so disreputable girls attract undesirable suitors. Their attention is specifically drawn to the stigma attached to pre-marital pregnancy. This causes eyebrows to be raised, tongues to wag, and the heads of unmarried mothers to be bowed in shame. The transition from adolescence to adulthood, the girls are told, is fraught with demanding challenges. Hence the guidance they are given and the lessons they are taught in the vhusha, and later the domba lodges.

The ten girls we found in the vhusha hut had already undergone four days of initiation. In addition to the tasks that had been set and the instruction received, they had also been practising vhusha dances at nights. At the command of the overseers, they rose from the floor, slunk out of the hut and began dancing in the courtyard to the beat of two drums. At

The great *vhusha* hut

first they danced in pairs, leaping, swirling and stamping their feet. Then later, with arms folded and bodies bent forward, they danced around the courtyard hearth, shuffling their feet and singing a lively *vhusha* ditty.

'This is how they will dance during the next two days, until the *vhusha* ends,' explained one of the overseers.

'Except that on the last day they have to do much more than dance,' said the second one, 'because then they are about to return to their homes. We wake them early, even before the sun has risen and, as has been the routine since they came to the lodge, we walk them to the stream in the valley. They walk one behind the other, one of them beating a drum as a warning for the village males not to come too close, because the girls must not be seen by males.

'When we arrive at the stream, they have to get into the water straight away, and bath for a very long time. Which is not pleasant for them, because it's cold at this time of the year. When they are dry, we shave their heads and then later they smear their bodies with fat. We stay a long time at the river,

but when we get back to the *vhusha* lodge, we spend even more time talking to them, and reminding them about the things we taught them during the past five days.

'The last night of the *vhusha* is the hardest of all for the girls, because they have to start dancing soon after dark, and continue with very little rest until the sun comes up. They are then taken to their homes, where they are welcomed back by their parents, and given food and new clothes and ornaments.

'And this is not the end of this initiation,' the overseer reminded us, 'they still have to attend the *domba*.'

Mulaudzi, the councillor and I remained in the lodge until the *vhusha* girls had finished dancing. During the rest of the day, we visited different parts of the royal village, calling on some of the older folk and discussing Venda history with them as well as various aspects of Venda culture. At sunset, Mulaudzi and I returned to Sibasa. Next morning, after breaking camp, we parted, having agreed to meet again towards the end of September.

The initiates dance around the *vhusha* hut

At the end of the dance the initiates file out of the
lodge bound for the nearby stream

The Domba

When I returned to Venda three weeks later, I found Mulaudzi in the cattlefold beside his home. On this occasion I had brought Harold, my twelve-year-old son, with me, and I introduced him to the children of Mulaudzi's village. He soon became involved in their various activities – playing hide and seek with them, following them as they charged after cattle that had strayed into the bush, climbing trees, wrestling, riding calves and thoroughly enjoying the pranks they played on each other. When the time came to leave and pitch camp near by, he was crestfallen and begged to be allowed to remain with his newly-found friends until sundown.

When the spring rains have fallen in Venda, the nights are cool and fresh with the scents of the countryside. On my return in September 1960, however, the veld, villages and bush were still laden with dust, and the air after dark was unmoving, hot and stale for want of rain. Sitting beside the campfire, Harold and I – Mulaudzi had decided to sleep at his home – could see puffs of lightning silently at play in the east, and I remember looking up into a clear, starry sky and wondering if the storm would reach us. We were to report to Chief Nelwamondo's hilltop village in the morning, when I would discuss the *domba* initiation ceremony with him and witness a display of dancing by the inmates of the *domba* lodge. Considering the ruggedness of the area, I realized that reaching the village would be difficult, if not impossible, in rainy conditions. I prayed for a sunny, cloudless dawn.

When we climbed into our sleeping bags at about ten o'clock, the stars had disappeared behind an umbrella of cloud, and the air, stirred by a gentle breeze, carried a musky smell of moistened dust. A wind sprang up, and whirling around us sprayed our camp with sand, leaves, grass and twigs. Then directly above us great whips of lightning began to lash the sky, crackling, thundering and finally unleashing a hailstorm that tore through the countryside.

In southern Africa, electric storms seldom last for long. This one was over within twenty minutes. As if by some mysterious intervention, the wind dropped, the lightning and thunder retreated and vanished, and the hail was replaced by a steady drizzle. Slowly I sank into a shallow slumber, and into my mind came a picture of Chief Nelwamondo's village. It was a curious scene: the living quarters were still dry and dusty, and yet in the *khoro* the rain was falling. Near the cattlefold gates the *domba* girls, clothed in blankets, sat huddled together defiantly refusing to dance. I could see myself sadly shaking my head. The ceremony had to be cancelled.

When I awoke dawn had broken. It was a hot, misty morning with low-hanging clouds, a faint drizzle and no trace of the rising sun. I made a fire from wood I had stored beneath a square of canvas, and placed a pot of water among the flames. Harold joined me soon afterwards, and while we were making coffee Mulaudzi arrived. He urged us to hurry lest we keep Chief Nelwamondo waiting, so we packed a hamper of fruit and biscuits, collected my cameras and other equipment and set out westwards across the hills.

The dusty track we had followed in August was muddy and slippery now, and littered with stones sluiced down the slopes. In parts, it had been washed away or was sheeted with water. Much of it was almost impassable.

We arrived at the trading store at the foot of Nelwamondo's hill with our truck bespattered and hissing steam, and continued on foot along the path that led to the chief's royal village. The higher we climbed, the thicker the mist became, and the drizzle although barely discernible played over our faces and oilskin cloaks. It was a tricky walk so I had to watch each step I took for fear of slipping and falling and damaging my cameras.

Within a stone's throw of the village palisades we picked up the sound of drums, and when we reached the gateway we were loudly hailed by a party of men. A councillor met us and led us through the *khoro* in the centre of which was a smoky fire. Close by were two short, forked poles that had been firmly planted in the *khoro* floor. These supported a cross-beam and a hanging, pot-bellied drum. We squelched through gluey mud to the opposite side of the *khoro*, entered Nelwamondo's courtyard and waited beneath the *marulla* tree. About twenty minutes later we were summoned by the chief and shown into his home, where we found him seated in a high-back chair.

'So you've remembered my invitation to come to the *domba*,' he grinned.

'Yes,' I replied, 'not even the rain and the mists could keep us away.'

'Rain!' he exclaimed. 'Rain is good during *domba* time, provided of course it is not too heavy, or continues too long, or is dangerous because of lightning. And it is even better if the rain should come at the close of the *domba*, because then we have other important things to think about, such as tilling our lands and planting our crops.

Zulu beehive huts. By contrast the inland tribes
build rondavel homes

The *domba* drummers

The male superintendent of the lodge beating the
ngoma drum

'Have you been to a *vhusha* lodge?' asked the chief, 'because this is what I meant to suggest to you.'

'Yes, I have,' I replied, 'I attended the *vhusha* at Chief Phiriphiri's old village.'

'And how much do you know about the *murundu*?' He was referring to the initiation ceremony for Venda boys.

'Not much,' I admitted, 'except what I have read about it, and what I have learnt from Mulaudzi and others.'

'Then you must get to know the *murundu* better,' continued the chief, 'for how else will you understand our way of preparing boys for adulthood? The very fact that our boy initiates are brought to the *domba*, and taught what it means to be a decent husband and father, makes it important for you to visit not only the *domba*, as you are doing today, but also the *murundu*. This you will have to do.

'Now let us talk about the *domba*,' said Nelwamondo, 'so that when I take you presently to the *khoro* where the initiates are, you'll better understand what's going on.

'I must explain from the start that the *domba* isn't held in my village every year. In fact, there hasn't been a *domba* here since 1956. This is because we have to wait for enough girls to pass through the *vhusha*, thirty or fifty and sometimes more; that is, girls who are almost old enough for betrothal and marriage. Then there are other considerations, such as the question of food. There's no sense in opening a lodge in the village if the harvests are poor, because it's possible for the *domba* to last for a year. No, the initiates and their overseers have to be looked after in every way, and they must be properly fed.

'The *domba* is always held in the village of a chief or headman, and is always superintended by an elderly man and a middle-aged female assistant. They are helped from time to time by maidens of the village, who have passed through a *domba* in years gone by. And the success of the *domba* depends to a large extent on the experience, authority and wisdom of the superintendent. He has to be a man of many parts – a firm disciplinarian, an outstanding instructor and a patient adviser. Above all, he has to be a person who likes young people, and in turn is liked and respected by them.'

The chief was interrupted by the sudden beating of drums in the *khoro* and the sound of singing and cheering.

'Ah!' he exclaimed. 'They've started at last, so you see not even rain or mist can prevent your seeing the dancing today. In the meantime, I will describe the *domba* to you from the day it opens until the day it closes. There's still plenty of time for us to talk, because the initiates will have to dance for at least two hours.

'On the first day of the *domba*,' he began, 'the initiates are assembled in the public hut. After dark, the *khoro* fills with women; not only the older ones, but also the maidens who took part in the last *domba* held here in the village.

'The *domba* girls are kept out of sight, in the hut, where eventually they are joined by the older maidens. All of them, including the maidens, then strip to nakedness, keeping on only the little apron worn by females during initiation. The initiates smear their bodies with ash and red clay, helping each other; and later when all the older women have come together around the hut, the girls are given porridge to eat. Some time after midnight they are given their first lesson in the python dance, a very beautiful but difficult dance, as you will presently see when we go to the *khoro*. It is also the most important dance of the *domba*; which is why lessons begin on the very first night.

'They continue to dance until sunrise. By then they are exhausted, and are taken back to the public hut and allowed to rest. Here they are addressed by some of the older people, who have much advice to give them. Afterwards they are given food and dismissed for the rest of the day. Craving sleep, they return to their homes, or to the homes of friends or relatives. Those that come from far-off parts, and have no place to go to, sleep in the *domba* lodge.

'On the second night, after a thorough rest, the girls assemble at the public hut where they are made to sit down close together, in a long line, one behind the other, and legs apart. Now lessons begin, the first of many they will receive in the months ahead on sex, betrothal, marriage, child-bearing and parenthood. This goes on right through the night, the older maidens dancing occasionally. And when the morning comes, the girls are examined by the assistant superintendent and other women to make sure they are virgins. For there is no greater disgrace than for a girl to have been deflowered before *domba* time. I am told that in some areas, this practice no longer exists, which I think is a pity. In our *domba*, an "unclean" girl is not only ridiculed, but also punished. She can't be excused, no matter what she says, because for many years she has been taught by her mother and, indeed, the overseers at the *vhusha* lodge, about the importance of remaining a virgin.'

The noise from the *khoro* had grown steadily louder. Above the drumming, singing and cheering rose the rhythmical clapping of hands interspersed with sporadic whistling

The dance performed by the married women of
Headman Moloto's village

The youngest initiate plays the small *ngoma* drum

and outbursts of laughter. So Mulaudzi, the councillor and I moved closer to the chief, to spare him having to raise his voice unduly. Nelwamondo seemed not to be bothered by the hubbub. Shifting to the edge of his chair and leaning forward, he continued to describe the proceedings and principles of the *domba*.

On the third day of the ceremony, he said, the *domba* began in earnest. It opened with a dance performed specifically in honour of the ancestors, to solicit their blessing. Meanwhile, the *domba* fire was laid and kindled in the *khoro* by a medicine man. In former years it was kept burning continuously throughout the duration of the *domba*, and had to be regularly fed with logs by selected attendants. But in the course of time, this age-old rule had been relaxed, Nelwamondo said, although the fire must always be relit by a medicine man. The *khoro* fire was the central point of the entire lodge. Around it most of the dancing and other activities occurred, month after month, until the *domba* was finally closed.

At nightfall on the third day the girls were joined for the first time by male initiates, and the entire group was escorted into the public hut and inducted into the routine and rules of the lodge. The initiates were told of the punishment they could expect should they transgress or dare to be lethargic, obstinate, sulky or disobedient. They were also made aware of a large number of unfamiliar words and phrases that were exclusive to the *domba*, and which had to be memorized and spontaneously used. Henceforth even their conversation would be subject to disciplines. For example, everyday words such as *khoro*, fire, gates, drums, beer, ash and huts were strictly taboo, and replaced by exotic *domba* terminology. So, until the close of the lodge, the slightest oversight, a mere slip of the tongue, would be met with some form of punishment.

The initiates were warned, the chief concluded, to be alert, punctual and quick in reacting to all commands. A drum was beaten each morning at daybreak, and they would have to assemble immediately. They then had to attend to chores such as sweeping the lodge, fetching water and firewood and cleaning cooking utensils. Afterwards they worked in the lands near the village, or were allotted to families who needed their help in repairing homesteads, cattlefold palisades, courtyard walls and threshing floors. In the afternoons, the drum was beaten again, summoning them back to the lodge. From then until bedtime they were given lessons in dancing, as well as in the conduct expected of them in various adult roles. This was the daily routine until the *domba* closed. It would be interrupted, however, from time to time in order to subject the initiates to tests of endurance. They would be made to sit flat on the ground, and then to cross the full length of the *khoro* without the support of their hands. They would also be made to pluck burning coals from the *domba* fire using only their fingers.

Chief Nelwamondo now suggested we repair to the *khoro* to watch the dancing. As we stepped out into the courtyard we found that the rain had stopped. The mist, however, had thickened, and a chill pervaded the air.

The *khoro* swarmed with people – women snuggled in blankets, men in overcoats, scores of half-clad maidens from previous lodges and fifty-one female initiates. Wearing no more than a modest apron, the *domba* girls were performing the python dance, their bodies moist from the heavy mist, and shining in the glow of the flames. Silhouetted in the smoke of the fire was the tall, statuesque figure of the elderly superintendent. Close by, his female assistant was beating the hanging, pot-bellied drum, and to the right of her were three initiates each playing a smaller one. Beside the fire lay a huge, tawny dog which jumped to its feet and angrily showed its teeth at us. I unpacked three of my cameras and slung them around my neck. The dog, I noticed with relief, had lost interest in us, and had lain down again to sleep.

The dancers were packed tightly together in a long, tapering line, the tallest in front and the shortest behind. Elbows bent, each girl had hold of the wrists of the one immediately in front of her, so that all the forearms were linked to create the impression of an enormous snake. In time to the beat of the drums, they moved gracefully around the *khoro* fire in a counter-clockwise direction. Each step they took was in perfect precision. And all the while the line of arms flowed smoothly upwards and downwards, forming a succession of arches and troughs in imitation of an advancing python.

Standing with his back to the fire, the superintendent led the initiates in singing the song of the python dance:

'The python unwinds itself…the snake unwinds,' he chanted, raising his falsetto voice above the thud of the drums.

'Ehé…ehé…,' the girls replied melodiously, over and over.

'The python unwinds…glides around the fire,' he quavered.

'Ehé…ehé…ehé…ehé.'

'Unwound…not resting, gliding, gliding.'

'Ehé…ehé…ehé…ehé.'

'Slowly, silently it winds in and out.'

'Ehé…ehé…ehé…ehé.'

After about half an hour, the drumming suddenly ceased and then restarted, switching to a more lively beat. The python dance was over. In the same position, arms still linked, the girls immediately picked up the new rhythm and broke into a quick-stepping dance. Now they moved rapidly round and round the fire, bodies swaying and, at a sign from the leader, would suddenly release their neighbours' wrists, fling up their arms, clap their hands four times above the head and then link up again. Often they would turn about face, re-establish the line in a flash, and then proceed in the opposite direction.

The singing was now being led by the tallest girl:

'Long ago we were staying at our parents' place,' she crooned.

'But now we are initiates of the *domba*,' came the reply in chorus.

'We are initiates, and therefore not yet ready to marry.'

'Not yet ready…but the day will come when we leave the *domba*…and find husbands and go to live with them.'

When this dance was over, the girls switched again to the slow, deliberate rhythm of the python dance. Ten minutes later, the superintendent brought the morning's proceedings to a close. The initiates fell on to their knees and, as a token of respect, bent forward until their foreheads came to rest on the ground. Given permission to sit up, they relaxed beside the fire, coyly conversing in whispers. A little later the superintendent dismissed them; they jumped to their feet and repaired in silence to the public hut.

Chief Nelwamondo now left the *khoro* taking Harold with him, so Mulaudzi and I ambled over to the fire where he introduced me to the superintendent.

'You have come on a very bad day,' said the superintendent, shaking my hand. 'Not only bad because of the weather, but bad because the dancing was poor.'

'I thought the girls danced beautifully,' I replied, 'and the photographs I took should come out well, in spite of the heavy mists.'

'They danced badly,' he retorted, 'and will have to be punished, even though it was not really their fault. They were upset because just before you arrived with the chief in the *khoro*, I had chased all the male initiates away. They had been playing the fool and showing off, making the girls giggle. So tonight they will all be made to dance much longer than usual, and tomorrow they will be woken up well before dawn to dance again.'

I had wondered what had become of the male initiates.

The python dance

After the slow python dance the initiates move
rapidly around the *domba* fire

The superintendent turned his attention to two maidens
carrying a bucket of water between them. Bowing before
him, they upturned the biggest drum and poured water into it
through a hole at the bottom. After thoroughly shaking the
drum, they held it erect, allowing the water to trickle out.
This I discovered was common practice. Being played so
close to the fire during the lengthy dance, the instrument
became hot and was liable to crack. It had always to be cooled
in this way.

When the maidens left, I had a close look at the drums.
They were beautifully made, each carved from a trunk of the
marulla tree. The biggest of the four, the hanging drum, was
approximately a metre in diameter. Known as the *ngoma*, it
was adorned around the upper part with four elongated
wooden handles into which a succession of exotic designs had
been cut. The shell of this drum was about two centimetres
thick, and was daubed with a mixture of red ochre and fat. An
ox-hide velum had been firmly pegged to the outer rim of
the mouth.

The three remaining drums consisted of a smaller *ngoma*
and two funnel-shaped *marimba*. During the dancing the
ngoma had been struck with heavy, rounded sticks, producing
a deep, booming sound. The tone of the *marimba*, on the
other hand, was high-pitched and crisp. They had been held
between the players' legs, and the tympana beaten with flat
hands and the finger tips.

While I was inspecting the drums, the rain came sluicing
down again, so Mulaudzi and I bade the overseer a hasty
farewell and headed for Chief Nelwamondo's home. We
discovered he had had a meal of roasted goat ribs, maize
porridge and beans prepared for us, and had already shared a
platterful with Harold. During lunch, the rain suddenly
stopped, and the sun came out. Knowing that the chief was
accustomed to an afternoon nap, we left him and retraced our
steps down the hill. By the time we reached our truck, there
was not a cloud in the sky, and I reflected on the inferior light
in which I had photographed the *domba* dances. I comforted
myself with the thought that some of my best photography
among the tribes of southern Africa had been taken under
worse conditions.

INITIATION FOR BOYS

The Thondo

Having been admitted to the *vhusha* and *domba* lodges, I was determined to follow Chief Nelwamondo's advice and make a study of initiation ceremonies for Venda boys. Mulaudzi suggested we spend the following day at Mbilwi, village of Chief Raluswielo Mphaphuli. Mbilwi, he explained, was conveniently situated near Sibasa but, more important, some of the village boys had recently returned from the *murundu*, a cirumcision lodge in the area. Besides, one of the chief's councillors, Headman Nemagovhani, had been a leading figure at the *murundu* lodge. A resident of Mbilwi, he was experienced and gifted with wisdom, and would prove to be an outstanding respondent. So we called on the chief in the morning, and with his permission sought out the headman. We found him in the village *khoro*.

Meeting Nemagovhani was a pleasing experience. When he recognized Mulaudzi and learned I had questions to ask him about the *murundu*, he took us by the arm, led us to a bench beneath the *khoro* tree, pulled up a chair and, sitting down, grinned at us with a generous spread of tusky teeth. He then offered us sorghum beer, which he scooped from a pot beside him. He was an elderly man, white haired, grey-bearded and heavily wrinkled. He had a catchy laugh, mischievous eyes and an engaging personality. In some ways, he reminded me of Sipho Mncube, my childhood friend.

'We should not discuss the *murundu* lodge and circumcision,' Nemagovhani said, turning his craggy face towards me, 'until we have first spoken about the *thondo* and *vhutambo vhutaka*. We have to look at initiation as a potter looks at making a pot – beginning at the bottom and working to the top. And just as the designing, polishing and baking is left for last, so the *murundu* is the final stage in initiation for boys.

'Many years ago, when I was about seven years old, I had to attend the *thondo* along with other boys from this area. We were taken by our fathers to a hut in a valley not far from here. It was a very big hut, wide and high, and around it was an even higher wall to make sure that we could not be seen from outside. That wall was important, because what happened in the *thondo* lodge was known only to men and to youths who had already been through initiation there. The lodge was a place that women, girls and even boys who were younger than ourselves were not permitted to visit.

'Now, during the day we initiates were allowed to herd our fathers' goats and cattle, to attend to the milking at home and

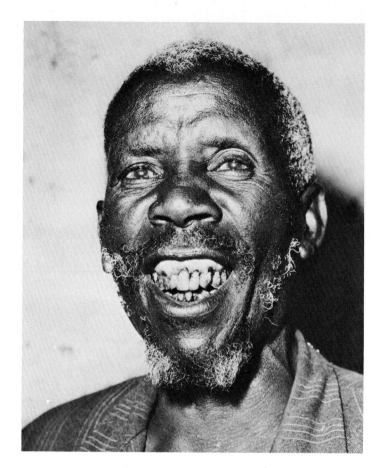

Headman Nemagovhani

even to play in the streams. But at nightfall we had to report to the lodge, where we were given lessons by the overseers in good behaviour, with a view to turning us into respectable youths. We were also given tasks to do, many of them so very difficult and painful that we often cried, wishing we could return to our homes. But as time passed and we began to succeed we grew less afraid, and felt proud of our bravery and growing strength.

'But nothing at the *thondo* was ever easy. We were regularly beaten, even for the smallest things such as whispering to each other when we were supposed to be quiet, or smiling when we were expected to be serious, or scratching an itch away when we were meant to be standing still. Often late at night, when we were in bed in the *thondo* hut, I would lie awake and think of home, and then fall asleep knowing I

Maize being sorted for the stamping block and
stamped into meal for baking maize cakes

A Venda village south of the Soutpansberg range

The communal drinking pot, Venda tribe

could not be released from initiation until the right time had come. I had a long time to wait, because the right time meant having to be about twelve years old.

'I remember becoming suddenly aware one day that my pubic hairs had started to grow. That was a sign that the time for leaving was near. I also clearly remember the day I was told by one of the overseers to report to him as soon as I had had my first wetness in sleep. He asked me if I knew what this meant, and I said I did. I had learnt about this kind of dream from the older boys.

'Then one night it happened. I had been dreaming about making love, and waking suddenly discovered the wetness the overseer had spoken about. So when the morning arrived I reported to him. He smiled at me and, placing his hand on my shoulder, said: "My son, you will soon be leaving the *thondo* lodge." I was allowed to leave about a month later. Not alone, but with other boys who had also reported their dreams.'

Old Nemagovhani now reached for the beer pot and, lifting it to his mouth, took a lengthy draught. He then passed the pot to Mulaudzi, wiping his lips and moustache.

'What I have told you so far happened very long ago,' he said, gathering his thoughts, 'many years ago.' And yet I can see myself as an initiate, as if I had never grown old. Initiation is something one never forgets. It's the hardest time in a person's life.

'How well I remember coming home from the *thondo*, and feeling proud that I would no longer be considered an ordinary child. And then, all of a sudden, came the time for the *vhutambo vhutaka*, which meant I was to become an initiate all over again, and be kept in a lodge with other boys.'

Vhutambo Vhutaka

'*Vhutambo vhutaka*,' the headman continued, 'means to wash away boyhood, and this "washing" was done by a group of unfriendly, past initiates under the supervision of elderly men. It took six long days to complete, from very early each morning to very late each night. It was hard. For example, we were given lessons on good manners, plenty of lessons on how to behave as youths and, in later years, as husbands, fathers and men of the tribe. And often while we were being taught these things, even if our manners were good we were beaten just to make sure they didn't get bad. That was hard, but harder still were the many hours we were made to sit in the wintry waters of the river, our bodies shaking all over from the cold and our teeth chattering, and the overseers beating us if we shivered too much or too little. It was difficult to know just how much to shiver.

'There were nights when we were so very tired and sleepy that we could have fallen asleep standing up, but we were forced awake by having to dance and dance, and then to work in the lodge before going to bed. That kind of hardship was so difficult to bear that when we thought of the river, and how much we had shivered, we wondered if the water was so cold after all. Nothing can be harder for a child, not even the cold, than to crave for sleep and yet be made to stay awake until you feel you are about to collapse.

'When the *vhutambo vhutaka* came to an end and the lodge was closed and we returned to our families, I was glad to think I was no longer a child. The younger children looked up to me, and I felt important even though I knew that in the eyes of adults I was no more than a boy. So I wondered when the next *domba* would be taking place, telling myself that this would be the last time I would have to undergo initiation. When once I had been through the *domba* I would be regarded as a man, and that was what I wanted to be. I had to wait five years before a *domba* could be arranged by our chief. I married soon after it came to an end.'

Circumcision

Stretching his arms and yawning luxuriously, Nemagovhani rose from the bench, picked up the earthen pot and called a maiden to fetch it and bring us more sorghum beer. Two elderly patriarchs had meanwhile entered the *khoro*. They had apparently been summoned by Chief Mphaphuli and as the headman of the village, it was Nemagovhani's duty to announce their arrival. So he left us with an assurance he would not be long.

Nemagovhani returned about an hour later and, finding us listening to a recording I had made of his voice, quietly sat down on the bench. He was fascinated. A talkative man, he became even more talkative now. So when I had played the tape through to the end, and replaced it with a new one, I asked him to tell us about circumcision in Venda and to describe the routine of the *murundu* lodge in which circumcised boys were housed.

Preparing maize cakes

Opposite Sandanu the *ramalia* (father) of the circumcision lodge

Tshikororo the *murundu* medicine man

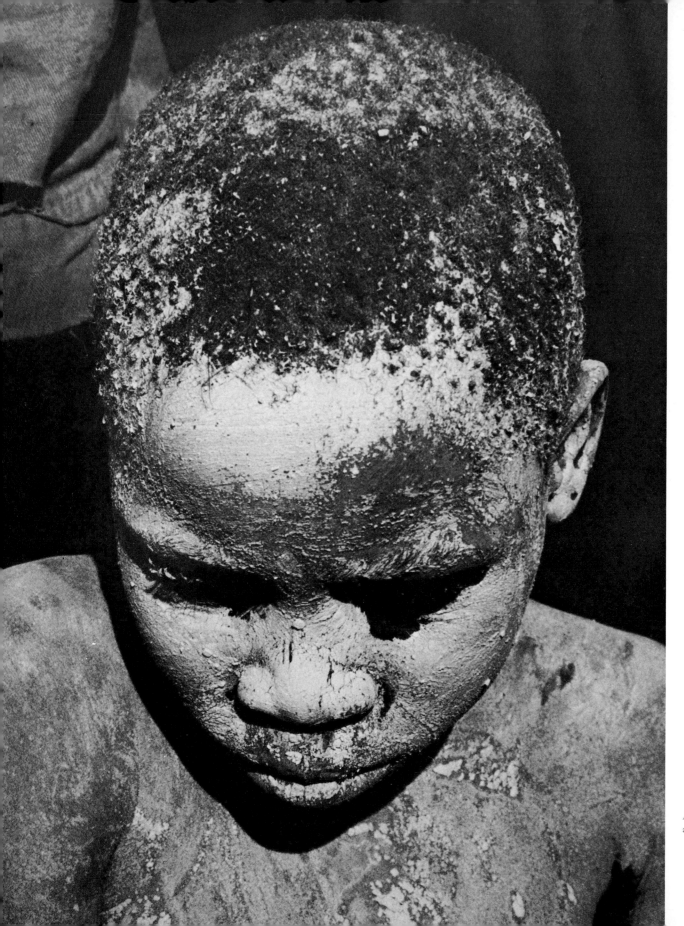

A *murundu* initiate
after circumcision

'Ah, the *murundu*!' the headman exclaimed. 'This gives us much to talk about. When my father was a boy, there was no *murundu*, no circumcision in Venda, and even when I was a boy it had hardly been heard of.

'I don't know exactly when the *murundu* became popular, but I remember that by the time I was no longer a very young man, boys were being sent from here and elsewhere to be circumcised in far-off parts of the country. And because there has always been so much secrecy about circumcision, it was difficult to find out how it came to Venda. Some of the older men used to say it was taught to us by our neighbours, the Tsonga and Sotho tribes, and others said it was started by the few Lemba people who settled among us. The important thing is not how or why the *murundu* developed in Venda, but what it meant to the initiation of boys: it slowly took the place of the *thondo* and *vhutambo vhutaka*. In fact, the *thondo* has now completely died out, and from what I am told, you have to go to the farthest hills to find a *vhutambo vhutaka* lodge. Today it is the custom for all our boys to be circumcised. Verily, should a youth reach adulthood without having been to a *murundu* lodge, he is considered a coward and cheat and one to be scorned. As I have said, circumcision was not widely practised when I was a child, but even so, to avoid disgrace, I myself had the operation done before I married.'

Headman Nemagovhani explained that the *murundu* was held every four or five years and had to be convened by a chief. This happened when it was brought to the ruler's notice that a large number of boys in his area needed to be circumcised. Invariably, he himself would have sons, and sometimes grandsons, who were eligible for circumcision, and would be keen for the organizers of the *murundu* to proceed with arrangements. Soon a site for the ceremony would be selected in a secluded spot. Then a team of workers would be mustered, and the lodge built.

'The *murundu* never opens until the harvests have been reaped and stored,' said Nemagovhani, 'and news of the appointed day spreads quickly to every village in the area ruled by the chief. Meanwhile, elders are appointed to stay in the lodge and serve as overseers. The two most important officials are the *ramalia*, who acts as the father in charge of the boys, and the medicine man who does the circumcising. In addition, many *midabe* are summoned to the lodge. They are youths who have passed through previous *murundus*, and are now required to supervise the boys and assist the overseers. This will give you some idea of how many people are housed in a *murundu* lodge – especially since there are at least twice as many initiates as elders and supervisors counted together.

'Now I have often been a *murundu* elder,' continued the headman with undisguised pride, 'and few people know better than I do how a lodge should be built. First of all, when the site has been chosen, it has to be blessed by a medicine man. It has to be big, because on one side we put up the huts of the initiates and young supervisors, and on the other, quite a distance away, those of the elders, the *ramalia* and the medicine man. In the middle of the lodge, running almost from the top end to the bottom, is the hearth where a fire is kept always burning, night and day, until the *murundu* comes to an end. Around the entire lodge, hiding the huts from the eyes of strangers, is a hedge built of thornbush branches. This is very long, high and thick, and has only two gateways – one to the side of the elders' section and the other close to the initiates.

'On the opening day of the *murundu*, as the initiates arrive with their fathers, they are assembled outside the lodge, not far from the gateway they will be using in the months ahead. But they cannot see the gateway, because it is crowded with the young supervisors and other people. No females, by the way; not a mother or grandmother or sister or aunt. No women at all. And the initiates don't really know what to expect. They certainly don't know they are about to be circumcised.

'This may surprise you, but you must understand that previous initiates have never been known to talk either to boys or women about the secrets of the *murundu*. No, a circumcised man or youth would never do such a thing, because he knows if he did he would be condemned, and classed as a kind of traitor. He also knows he would be exposed to endless misfortune, or even to death at the hands of the ancestral spirits.

'When the time comes for the circumcising to begin, the medicine man arrives at the gateway and is given a seat just outside the lodge. The young supervisors form a circle around him, and start making a noise, loudly singing, shouting and beating drums. Meanwhile the medicine man has placed a leather bag at his feet, and from it he takes a few sharpened assegai blades. The noise grows louder, and louder still when suddenly the first initiate is brought into the circle, and is told to sit on a big, flat stone in front of the medicine man.

'Just imagine what goes on in the minds of the boys as one by one they are circumcised. Most of them are only about ten years old, and have therefore not seen much of human blood.

They scream when they suddenly see the bloody stone, and continue to scream as they are held by the medicine man's helpers and circumcised. Not for long though, because the medicine man works very fast, and they realize there's no point in screaming when they can't be heard in the noise around them. And of course the noise the overseers make is important for another reason: it prevents an initiate's screams being heard by the unsuspecting boys who have still to be circumcised.

'The wounds are immediately dressed with medicinal leaves which the medicine man has had collected in the hills by the overseers. Then the initiates, limping from the pain, are led to a place not far from the gateway. They are given moist, white clay by the overseers and told to smear it all over their bodies, from the top of their heads to their toes. Later, when they have all been circumcised, bandaged with leaves and properly covered with clay, they are taken for the first time into the *murundu* lodge, and shown their living quarters.

'They are nervous and look very sad as they enter the huts, and are told to sit down and rest. And for a while you can hear them crying and sniffing, and then becoming quiet, trying their best to be brave. For the remainder of the day, they continue to rest; but at nightfall they are called from the huts, given a quick meal of dry porridge and assembled near the *murundu* fire, where they watch a display of dancing by the elders and overseers. When bedtime comes, they are all so tired, that falling asleep comes easily.'

The headman stood up now, complaining that his back was sore, his stomach empty and his mouth parched from all the talking. He would not be able to continue, he said, until he had had something to eat, so he intended to join the chief and the visiting patriarchs in order to share a meal with them. He asked us to wait for him in the *khoro*, promising he would not be long.

He was back within twenty minutes, accompanied by Chief Mphaphuli, the patriarchs and an elder of the village called Masia. Inviting them to sit down beside us in the shade of the *khoro* tree, he then returned to his seat and continued to talk about the *murundu*.

'After the first night in the lodge,' he began, 'the circumcised boys have a very strict routine to follow. Every morning, the young supervisors get up before sunrise, call the initiates from the huts and make them sit, one behind the other, in a circle around the *murundu* fire. Here announcements are made, instructions given for the day and punish-

ment meted out to boys who have disobeyed the rules of the lodge. The initiates are also regularly made to fetch burning coals from the fire, using only their hands, as a test of their ability to endure such pain.

'After the meeting at the fire comes the morning meal, which consists of cold, stiff, maize porridge and nothing else. This food is not cooked in the lodge. It is prepared in the villages, and taken by the initiates' mothers or elder sisters to a specially appointed place, where it is fetched by the *murundu* supervisors.

'As soon as they have eaten, the initiates smear white clay on to their bodies, making sure that no part of the skin shows through. Then they are taken into the valleys and hills to hunt, everyone carrying two sticks for throwing at hares, quails or partridges. They return with the supervisors at sunset, sit again around the *murundu* fire and practise the secret words and sayings of the lodge. This special *murundu* language must be thoroughly known by them within the first five days. After that, if they make mistakes, using words they are no longer allowed to use, the supervisors beat them.

'The evening meal comes after the period of learning beside the fire. It consists again of cold, stiff porridge, which is all the boys are given to eat until the *murundu* closes; yet day after day they eat hungrily. They become very thirsty. This is because of the time they have to spend in the sun or beside the fire, without a drop of water to drink. They are forced to do without water for at least a month...a difficult task when you're hot and thirsty and know there's a stream near by.

'Most nights a little dancing follows the evening meal, and then the boys are sent to their huts. No talking, no whispering as they lie down to sleep. Only the supervisors continue to talk.

'This routine doesn't change for about two months. Then one morning the boys wake up and discover that the supervisors have planted a long, smooth pole near the *murundu* fire. They are made to dance around the pole, and later to take turns in climbing it. This isn't easy, because the pole is slippery and twice as high as the *murundu* huts. On the top of the pole is a piece of skin, which has to be touched by the climbers before they are allowed to come down again. As each of the boys succeeds, he shouts for joy, and then proudly listens to the supervisors and initiates as they join in the shouting.

'From now on other changes take place at the lodge: now the boys are allowed to drink water, and when they come to sit around the *murundu* fire, as they have been doing each day,

Food brought to the *murundu* by the initiates'
mothers and sisters

Maize cakes delivered to the outskirts of the
circumcision lodge by some of the initiates' sisters

they find they have to face the opposite way, as if the old way had been wrong. Another change is that every morning, one of the initiates is made to dress in a long reed costume, and is sent with a supervisor to dance before the women who bring the food. He must not be recognized by them of course, so his face is covered with a plaited mask.

'A few days before the *murundu* closes, the three best dancers among the initiates are dressed in the same disguise, and taken by the supervisors into the veld where a crowd of men, women and younger people have gathered to watch them dance. This is a sign for the relatives of the boys that the *murundu* will soon be closing. It is a happy event, and is followed by everyone singing, dancing and cheering and really enjoying themselves.

'On the last night of the *murundu* a great feast is held in the lodge, to which all circumcised males in the district are expected to come. Next morning, the initiates are taken to the stream near by, and told to jump into the water and wash the clay from their bodies. Then their heads are shaved and their bodies smeared with fresh, red clay. Meanwhile the lodge has been set alight and everything used by the boys – clothing, blankets and sleeping mats – is thrown into the flames by a party of supervisors. The *murundu* is over. It is a thing of the past. So the boys are warned to make sure they don't look at the rising smoke, because this could cause them misfortune in the new life to come.

'Towards midday, all the initiates come together in a group. Hands held humbly in front of their chests, and heads bowed low, they follow the elders and young supervisors to the chief's village. There they are met by a gathering of the initiates' mothers, who quickly identify their sons, giving them tasty food to eat and newly made strings of beads to wear. It's a happy occasion, and the village fills with the noise of talking, laughing and singing and the beating of drums.

'*Murundu* time is full of surprises, and these can be very unpleasant, even during the welcoming ceremony. For just as the boys begin to feel happy for the first time since their circumcision, they are told they are not yet ready for home. "But why?" they ask, some of them wanting to weep. "Because you have to work for the chief," they are told, "in his lands and other parts of the village."

'So, when the welcoming is over, the boys are taken away, leaving the gathering to feast. During the following four, five or six days, depending on how long they are needed by the chief, they stay in the village working from early in the morning until dark. This kind of life isn't as hard as what went on in the *murundu*, but being freer now they complain and grouse among themselves, making sure they are not heard by the supervisors.

'They believe the chief takes more time than is necessary to be satisfied with the amount of work they have done. And yet when he calls them together and says they can leave, there are some initiates who find parting difficult.

'This is what living together, suffering together does for *murundu* boys. They become as one in loyalty to each other, to their elders and chiefs. They get to know what it really means to be a Venda.'

There is a saying that if a snuffing man takes pleasure in generously offering his snuff-box to friends, you can be sure he will be just as generous in other ways. Such a man, it is said, has a liking for people, and in enjoying their company is liked in return. Headman Nemagovhani was this kind of snuff-taking man. For although he had already spared us so much of his time, he insisted that Mulaudzi and I remain in the village until nightfall, and share the tranquillity of the *khoro* with him.

During the afternoon, he spoke no more about the *murundu*, except on one occasion when he assured me that had I come to the village three months earlier, he might have been able to show me a lodge. He treated us to a series of anecdotes gleaned from his life and the lives of chiefs, headmen and other dignitaries he knew. He was so entertaining that Chief Mphaphuli and the patriarchs remained with us until dusk, when we decided to leave. Still talking, Nemagovhani accompanied us to the truck, and as a parting gift, presented Mulaudzi with a rooster and me with the liver of a newly-killed goat.

No wonder the old headman's snuff-box could never stay full.

Venda Food

Mulaudzi and I spent the following three days at Mbilwi, Chief Mphaphuli's village, returning each night to our camp near Sibasa. With Nemagovhani's guidance, I was able to make a study of Venda dietary preferences. I watched the women preparing circular loaves from ground maize meal, and their daughters making patties from peanuts grown near the settlement. On two occasions I was treated to a stew made of miniature wild figs, wild spinach, beans and *mashonzhe* (caterpillars collected from *mopani* trees). In one of the

homesteads, I shared a meal of termites, flying ants, stiff porridge and gravy with the owner, and in another I enjoyed a plateful of rissoles made of finely ground locusts. I had sampled similar dishes among the Kwena (Crocodile People) of Botswana four years before, and had found them just as palatable. Had my opinion been asked on the taste of these foods, either in Botswana or Venda, I might have suggested they could be improved by adding pepper, and definitely an extra helping of salt.

Those last three days spent in the Mbilwi village were enough to convince me that the Venda relish a great variety of other foods – beef and goat's meat (although the slaughter of these animals was normally restricted to ceremonial occasions); the flesh and offal of wild birds and game (excluding predators); fish, poultry and dairy products. Eggs were considered a delicacy, but because of the aphrodisiacal properties attributed to them, had to be avoided by adolescent girls as well as maidens on the brink of betrothal.

This brief study brought our visit to Venda to a close. On departing for home, both Harold and I were sad at having to leave Mulaudzi, and I assured him I would try to return before harvest time.

'This will make the three of us happy again,' smiled Mulaudzi.

Molandwa the Herbalist

I had no opportunity to return to Venda until August 1969. I reached Sibasa on a Monday afternoon and drove straight to Mulaudzi's village, but I was shocked to learn on arrival that he had died some years before. Since our parting in 1960, I had written to him on four occasions, but had received only one letter from him in reply. According to a greybeard called Madula, whom I met at the village, Mulaudzi had become decrepit as the result of a lingering illness, and so had been unable to keep in touch with me. Madula added that he knew who I was, having often heard Mulaudzi talk about me. When I told him I had come to make a study of initiation for boys, he said he could arrange for a herbalist named Molandwa to accompany me to a *murundu* lodge in the north near Lake Fundudzi. He suggested that the herbalist and I seek an interview with the *ramalia* and medicine man, because only with their permission would I be able to see the *murundu* initiates and study their various activities.

I agreed to this, in order not to disappoint the old man, but privately I decided against the idea. One cannot arrive at a *murundu* uninvited or without prior permission from the local chief or the *ramalia*. I blamed myself for not having made proper arrangements before coming to Venda, and for assuming that Mulaudzi or one of my other Venda friends would be able to open the way to a *murundu* for me. I felt a little discouraged now, but then it suddenly occurred to me that, if he agreed, I could continue my study of indigenous medicines under guidance of Molandwa the herbalist. So everything depended on whether he would agree to accompany me.

As the greybeard was eager to introduce me to Molandwa, he suggested we set out for his home two kilometres to the west, and confer with him. We found the herbalist alone in his courtyard. He was very old, was hard of hearing and spoke with a stammer. When he learned I needed him to act as my guide, he seemed doubtful at first, pensively stroking his beard, but then taking my hand said he would be pleased to go with me.

'Molandwa is a very wise old man,' the greybeard said, presumably feeling I needed to be reassured, 'and so very knowledgeable in the ways of the Venda that you will learn far more from him than I could teach you. I have asked him when he would be ready to leave for the lake, and he has said straight away, if that's what you want.'

About twenty minutes later, having taken the greybeard back to Mulaudzi's village, Molandwa and I departed for Lake Fundudzi. We reached its southern shore as the sun was setting, pitched the tent, lit a fire under a *marulla* tree and cooked a stew from canned beef and vegetables. At dusk, we sat close together in the glow of the fire to eat and talk.

As Molandwa had been a *murundu* medicine man in years gone by, we discussed circumcision as it is practised not only in Venda but also among other tribes of southern Africa. He was amazed to find I had been admitted to lodges in Transkei, and was particularly interested in photographs I showed him of Bomvana, Tembu and Ngqika initiates. He asked me if I had photographed *murundu* boys during previous visits to Venda, and when I said I had not, he predicted I would do so one day.

In the clearing below the lodge girls sing to the beat of *marimba* drums

'But not soon,' he added, 'not this week, or next week or even this year.'

'Then when?' I ventured.

'Who can tell?' he replied. 'It all depends on when it is meant to be.'

For the next five days Molandwa and I scoured the wooded hills around the lake for time-tested medicinal bulbs, tubers, roots, tree bark, leaves, berries and fruits. We would return each evening, Molandwa carrying a digging adze and short-handled spade and I a bulging bag of specimens. Emptying the bag on to a canvas beside our tent, I would first sort out the items and then, with the help of my mentor, record their indigenous names as well as the ailments for which they were used.

Research of this kind can be fatiguing, considering the walking, climbing, searching, digging and carrying it demands. I had expected old Molandwa to start complaining after a day or two, but he was so energetic that it was sometimes difficult to convince him we needed to break for lunch. In fact, on the morning of the sixth day, after breaking camp, he nagged me to spend a further week with him in some other part of the territory.

'But are you not tired?' I teased.

'Tired!' he exclaimed indignantly. 'How can I be tired? I've spent my whole life collecting medicines and working with them, and all the time enjoying what I was doing. Tired? No. It is only when you have something to do that you don't like doing that you soon start getting tired. So soon sometimes, that you're feeling tired, needing to rest, even before you've started to work.

'But what about you?' he said smugly. 'Have we been working too hard since we came to the lake?'

'Not at all,' I assured him. 'I enjoy this work.'

'Then we can continue collecting?' he asked.

'Unfortunately no,' I replied. 'Because, as I told you a few days ago, I must be back at my home by tomorrow night.'

'And you'll be coming back?' he queried.

'For sure I will.'

'And we'll be working together again?'

'Just the two of us,' I nodded, 'and we'll enjoy it so much we'll never get tired.'

Spontaneously we embraced each other in a silent expression of happiness.

The Murundu Lodge

Five years later, at the beginning of July 1975, I set out for Venda again, this time accompanied by Lionel Friedberg and the television crew of Films of Africa. At Sibasa we acquired the use of a vacant bungalow and, having moved in with our film and camping equipment, made contact with a local dignitary named Mishack Madavha whom we persuaded to act as our guide. Middle-aged, balding and corpulent, Madavha was a quick-witted, jovial man. He was known to many of the chiefs and headmen, and had ready access to their villages.

With Madavha to open the way for us, we spent the first week filming various aspects of Venda culture in hilltop villages just north of Sibasa. Then he arranged for us to be admitted to *vhusha* and *domba* lodges in the area and, for almost a week, beginning each day at sunrise and ending late at night, we filmed the dances and other activities of the female initiates. Next, Madavha suggested we move to Duthuni, some twenty-five kilometres north-west of Sibasa, explaining that hundreds of circumcised boys had been housed in a *murundu* there since the beginning of June. The father, medicine man and elders had been informed about our presence in Venda, and had given permission for some of the activities of the lodge to be photographed for television.

I remembered the discussion I had had with old Molandwa the medicine man, five years before at Lake Fundudzi. Had he not predicted I would one day be coming into contact with *murundu* initiates; and did he not say I would have to wait until this was 'meant to be'? As things were turning out, I told myself, the lengthy wait had been worthwhile.

Friedberg, the camera crew, Madavha and I departed for Duthuni by truck on an immaculate Sunday morning. Having covered most of the distance along a winding mountain road, we then followed a narrow cattle track through bush, shrubs and elephant grass and the overhanging branches of white stinkwood trees. After struggling for some twenty minutes – at one stage we almost overturned the truck – we reached a clearing where we were told by Madavha to stop and off-load our equipment. I was surprised to find no sign of people. The clearing lay in the hollow of an encircling rise overgrown with thorntrees, scrub and thatch-

Having been confined to the lodge for several
weeks the initiates seemed puzzled at having been
brought into the clearing

Waiting for instructions from the *ramalia*

ing grass, and was traversed by a solitary footpath which apparently led to a distant village. Not a sound reached us from it. In fact, in the entire countryside we could hear no more than the chirping of finches and a remote cackling of guinea fowl.

According to Madavha, the *murundu* was situated to the right of us not far beyond the rise. As he expected the initiates to arrive very suddenly, he led us to a suitable vantage point and suggested we set up the cameras and prepare for filming.

We had just reached the spot selected by Madavha when I noticed a line of women coming down the footpath towards the clearing. Some bore baskets of grain on their heads and others earthen pots containing dome-shaped maize meal cakes. They were the mothers and sisters of *murundu* initiates, a few of the scores of women who visited the clearing each day, and left rations for the supervisors to collect and take to the boys. Having reached the edge of the clearing, the women squatted in the grass, and placed the baskets and pots before them in rows. Now they waited in silence, occasionally whisking flies away from the food with oxtail switches.

Ten minutes later we became aware of distant singing – a chorus of female voices accompanied by the thudding of drums. Soon afterwards a squad of at least one hundred *vhusha* and *domba* girls came streaming down the footpath towards us. Most of them were clad in no more than scanty aprons or loin cloths and small items of ornamentation. Entering the clearing, they came to a halt, formed up in a compact group and continued to sing. Next moment, a party of men appeared from out of the bush – headmen, councillors and *murundu* elders. They swaggered across the clearing, took up a position to the right of us, and sat down side by side, erect and motionless. A messenger arrived and signalled the *vhusha* and *domba* girls to stop singing and beating the drums. Announcing the approach of the *murundu* party – the *ramalia*, the medicine man, the initiates and their supervisors – he called upon everyone to stand up and wait in silence.

Suddenly a man appeared on the skyline; he had emerged from the other side of the rise. Holding a white flag above his head, he waved it repeatedly from left to right. Then came the sound of singing, and about a minute later the *murundu* party came into sight. Pausing briefly on top of the rise, it moved slowly down the slope towards us led by the man with the flag. Close behind him were the *murundu* father and medicine man, their heads adorned with skin headdresses and their torsos with leopard pelts. We could see no sign of the initiates. They were hidden from view by row upon row of supervisors pressed tightly together, shoulder to shoulder. Brandishing canes, the supervisors glared constantly in the direction of the women and girls, presumably on the look out lest one of them dared to sneak a glimpse at the *murundu* boys.

Meanwhile Lionel Friedberg, having photographed the women, the girls, the headmen and other dignitaries, turned his attention to the advancing procession. At first he seemed delighted with what he viewed through the lens and was capturing on film, but no sooner had the *murundu* party reached the foot of the slope than he switched off the camera complaining that the initiates were completely obscured. I wondered if we would in fact be permitted to photograph the newly circumcised boys, as I had done in the lodges of other tribes, and decided to introduce myself to the *ramalia* and discover what he and the medicine man had planned for us.

I had just started walking towards the clearing when a messenger arrived with news that the *ramalia* would soon be sending for us. He and the medicine man were at that moment conferring with the headmen, the councillors and elders of the lodge, the messenger said, so we must be patient knowing we had not been overlooked.

By now the man with the flag had led the *murundu* party into the centre of the clearing and, calling a halt, had positioned himself like a sentinel in the space between the boys and the womenfolk. The supervisors continued to sing, while the women and girls looked on impassively. I could see the headmen and other dignitaries happily conversing with the *ramalia* and medicine man, patting them on the back and shaking their hands.

After about half an hour we were fetched by the messenger and introduced first to the *ramalia*, then to the medicine man and finally to the man with the flag. Then we were taken by the *ramalia* into the centre of the *murundu* party, where we discovered about forty initiates, ranging in age from nine to thirteen years. Daubed all over with thick, white clay, they looked sad and bewildered, and appeared puzzled by our sudden intrusion on their privacy. They became apprehensive of Friedberg and the whir of his camera, and as I walked among them explaining the scene for television I could sense they were wondering who I was and what I was saying about them. They must have looked upon our visit as one of the most unusual experiences they had had since coming to the lodge. I would like to believe, however, that we succeeded in diverting their thoughts from some of the hardships they had been forced to endure as *murundu* initiates.

The *madagalane* arrive

Moving like phantoms around the clearing

The *madagalane* costume consists of three parts – a
plaited mask, a cape and skirt

As soon as we completed the filming the boys were taken up the slope and over the rise, and returned to the *murundu* lodge. Once again, they were carefully screened by the overseers to prevent the womenfolk from seeing them.

Silence fell over the clearing, then suddenly, in response to a signal from one of the elders, the girls began to sing and beat the drums. The food-bearers remained seated in rows beside their baskets and pots of maize meal porridge, while the headmen, councillors and other dignitaries drank sorghum beer which had been brought to them by female attendants. Friedberg and the camera crew waited close by in the shade of a tree. I remained in the centre of the clearing with the *murundu* father and medicine man. They had agreed to tell me about the role they played in the lodge, so we sat down close together with my tape recorder between us. I had almost completed my interview when the *murundu* dignitaries drew my attention to three phantom-like figures on the top of the rise. I sat up in astonishment then, realizing that the medicine man was laughing at me, I smiled sheepishly back at him.

'Those are the *madagalane*,' he said, 'the three best dancers among all the initiates. Recently they have been coming each day to the clearing to dance before the women and girls who bring food for the boys at the lodge. Next Sunday, the *murundu* will come to an end, so from now on the *madagalane* will have to dance more regularly, starting with a performance for the crowd that has gathered here.'

I recalled the discussion I had had with Headman Nemagovhani at the Mbilwi royal village about initiation among Venda males. He had told me about these special dancers, the *madagalane*, and the disguise they wore to avoid identification.

The three *madagalane* came slowly down the slope towards us, each in the charge of a supervisor; and as they swayed into the clearing I was taken by the *ramalia* and medicine man to have a closer look at their costumes. These were made entirely of reed and consisted of three main items – a thick, flowing skirt, an equally thick cape which extended from the neck to the waist, completely obscuring the torso, and finally a tall, conical, woven mask which fitted on to the shoulders and upper parts of the chest and back. The mask had no facial features, which meant the initiates had to see and breathe as best they could through gaps in the weaving.

The *madagalane*'s dance was far from impressive. They merely moved slowly forward, swinging now to the left and now to the right, their reed skirts floating and curling and encircling their bodies in rhythmical sweeps. They were accompanied by the supervisors, who steered them in various directions by gently tapping their shoulders with twigs. Back and forth they danced along the lines of food bearers, then round and round the group of singers, then across the clearing and finally up the nearby slope and over the rise.

'E-lé...e-lé...e-lé...e-lé...' The girls had been singing these words for the past half hour; monotonously, over and over in high-pitched voices, and loudly so as almost to drown the thud of the drums.

'E-lé...e-lé...e-lé...e-lé...' One wondered how the headmen, councillors and elders could hear themselves talk, and how long the singing would continue. I had found difficulty in conversing with the *murundu* father and medicine man, for they were soft-spoken men and had made no effort to raise their voices above the singing.

'E-lé...e-lé...e-lé...e-lé...' Since the departure of the three *madagalane* the girls had sung louder and faster, and were clapping their hands in time with the drums.

Then, suddenly, the singing turned into a confusion of shrieks and cries: 'The wildman! The wildman! Beware of the wildman!'

The wildman? Somewhat perplexed, I glanced around me. Who could this be; where was he hiding and why did the dignitaries in the clearing seem unconcerned?

In a matter of moments the hubbub stopped. The girls, I noticed, had fallen to the ground, and had buried their faces in their hands or arms. The food-bearers lay curled up beside the baskets and pots. No one moved, and an uneasy stillness pervaded the clearing.

Then I caught sight of the wildman, in the direction of the pathway beyond the prostrated girls. He came galloping down the slope, arms aloft, and was followed by three of the *murundu* supervisors. Covered in white clay, he wore a kilt and simple headdress, both of which were made of reeds. In his right hand he carried an assegai and battle-axe, and in his left two fighting sticks. One of his companions was similarly dressed. The others, although also stripped to the waist, were neither daubed with clay nor clad in kilts. Instead they wore short, tight-fitting trousers.

Reaching the bottom of the pathway, the wildman and his followers swerved to the left and came loping towards us. They sped past the girls, tore through the clearing and disappeared into the nearby bush. The girls then jumped to their feet, and fled screaming in the opposite direction. I watched in amazement as they scrambled up the pathway,

While the *madagalane*
dance, the overseers steer
them by tapping their
shoulders with twigs

The *madagalane* move on after dancing before the
food bearers

As the wildman appears on the scene the girls fall
to the ground and cover their faces

The mothers make sure not to set eyes on the
wildman

The wildman

bound for their villages and the sanctuary of their homes. They had been warned since childhood, I reflected, against venturing too close to *murundu* lodges lest they be captured and beaten by the supervisors. But what of the wildman; why had his sudden arrival caused them so much fear? I decided to ask the medicine man.

I learned that, by custom, one of the supervisors played the wildman's role. To Venda girls, however, he was a legendary figure, a fiendish creature that would cause them lasting misfortune should they intentionally or even inadvertently come face to face with it. They were taught about this wildman in infancy, and were consistently reminded about him, particularly during *murundu* time.

Today the girls had not expected him to appear. No wonder they were terrified.

When all the girls and women were out of sight the wildman and his attendants reappeared in the clearing, emerging from a thicket to the right of us. As they strolled towards us the wildman struck me as being a friendly young man: two of his companions had placed a hand on his shoulders and he smiled continuously as he chatted to them. Raising his assegai, he hailed the *ramalia*, the medicine man and the party of elders, and then sat down beside us. He readily agreed to my taking a series of photographs of him; and even when eventually the *ramalia*, the medicine man and the elders took leave of us, and moved out of the clearing, he remained behind to talk to Madavha. Indeed when we returned to our truck he accompanied us, and bade us a cordial farewell.

Memories of Venda will linger in the minds of Friedberg and the camera crew as surely as the place will dwell forever in mine. In Venda the luxuriance of nature is delicately tinctured in many hues, lavishly orchestrated with animal, bird and insect song and scented with the aroma of forests, the morning mists and the smoke of village cowdung fires. Venda has a charm that nurtures nostalgia, and yet as I release my thoughts over southern Africa, I see all tribal areas in similar light – the East Coast territories, the Western deserts, the bushveld flats and the hilly and mountainous regions that mother a host of inland tribes.

Index